Second Edition

Kayaking

THE BROKEN GROUP ISLANDS

on Canada's West Coast, Pacific Rim National Park Reserve

The Essential Guidebook

by JF Marleau

Pacific Rim Informative Adventures (PRIA)

Updated 2008

Printed in Canada

Published by
Pacific Rim Informative Adventures (PRIA)
Box 727, Ucluelet, BC V0R 3A0
www.priaoutback.com
info@priaoutback.com

National Library of Canada Cataloguing in Publication

Marleau, Jean-François, 1977–

Kayaking the Broken Group Islands on Canada's West Coast,
Pacific Rim National Park Reserve.
The Essential Guidebook / JF Marleau

Second Edition

ISBN 0-9739877-0-7

1. Sea kayaking — Pacific Rim National Park (B.C.) — Guidebooks.
2. Sea kayaking — British Columbia — Barkley Sound
Region (B.C.) — Guidebooks.

Cover photos:
Kevin Bradshaw, Wendy Szaniszlo and Barbara Schramm

Graphics and layout by Schramm Design

Written, edited and designed in Ucluelet, BC, Canada

CONTENTS _____ 3

Maps & Figures

DISCLAIMER

This guidebook can not replace outdoor experience, a book on kayak safety, or a professional kayaking course. Rather, it is designed to provide basic information to help paddlers plan their trip to the Broken Group Islands and to develop an awareness of the cultural and natural heritage of the islands.

Please note that travelling on the ocean or among the islands of Barkley Sound is inherently dangerous. You may encounter challenging navigation or weather conditions, unexpected vessel traffic, poor visibility, rugged terrain and wild animals. Use extreme caution when travelling in Barkley Sound waters. Paddling conditions may suddenly deteriorate due to weather and other factors. Sheltered waters may rapidly intensify into areas of extreme hazard.

Respect the power of the ocean.
Photo: Barbara Schramm

Pacific Rim Informative Adventures Ltd. and Jean-François Marleau assume no liability for any accidents, damage, injuries or death that may be sustained by anyone using the information provided in this book. Pacific Rim Informative Adventures Ltd. and Jean-François Marleau do not warrant that the waters of Barkley Sound are safe or that the information in this book is completely accurate. Therefore, please be careful when using this or any other source to plan and carry out your outdoor recreation activity. Paddlers travel at their own risk.

NOTICE TO READER:

Some kayaking guidebooks suggest day trip routes with distances and time estimates without taking into considerations important variables. Choosing a route for a day trip should be based on several variables which a guidebook can't predict. These variables include wind direction, wind speed, weather forecast, weather outlook, tides, swells, fog, currents, skills and knowledge of group members, expectations of group members, paddling speed of the group, as well as many other variables. This guidebook provides all the tools and information needed to assist in planning your daily route.

Acknowledgements

Many people have contributed to this book by sharing their time, knowledge or photos, or by supporting me and the development of this book in countless other ways. Most of these folks are from Ucluelet and are former or current employees of the Pacific Rim National Park Reserve. Thanks to Wendy Szaniszlo, Barry Campbell, Bob Hanson, Jill Brown, Brock Fraser, John McIntosh, Gord McClean, Doug Andrew, Alan Sobey, Brian Gisborne, Kevin Bradshaw, Bill Fox, Liz Johnson, Darren Salisbury, Andrew Woodford and Sea Kayak Instruction & Leadership Systems (SKILS).

My gratitude goes also to Wendy Szaniszlo, Frankie Allen and Greg Blanchette for editing this book; Barbara Schramm for layout, photos and design; and Frank Poulsen for the maps.

A special thanks go to Wendy Szaniszlo, Arlene Armstrong, Bill McIntyre, Dan Vedova, Mary Watson, Greg Blanchette and Silva Johansson for their advice and help with the revision of the contents. Their contribution was essential. Thanks also to Parks Canada and Pacific Rim National Park Reserve Archives for access to many historical photos.

— JF Marleau, Ucluelet, March 2008

Introduction

The Broken Group Islands (BGI) is one of the most famous sea kayaking destinations in the world. Its spectacular beauty and abundant diversity of wildlife offer a unique wilderness experience. The BGI, one of the three units of Pacific Rim National Park Reserve (PRNPR), has much to offer kayakers of all levels. The inner islands include sheltered waters and quiet lagoons, while the outer islands, where waves pound rocky shores, give a taste of the open ocean's strength and fury.

A rich variety of land and marine mammals, intertidal invertebrates, and birds live in this archipelago of over 100 islands and islets. When you visit the BGI you are visiting the traditional lands of the Nuu-chah-nulth peoples, whose history in this place spans the last 5,000 years.

Although kayaking is the main activity in the BGI, tidepooling, exploring the islands, and wildlife viewing will enhance your experience. The many beaches, the lush forests with their giant western red cedar trees, and the never-ending entertainment of watching sea lions will all add to your enjoyment.

Life is short, so enjoy every moment of it!

Sheltered waters offer great bird watching. Photo: Barbara Schramm

General information
about the Broken Group Islands

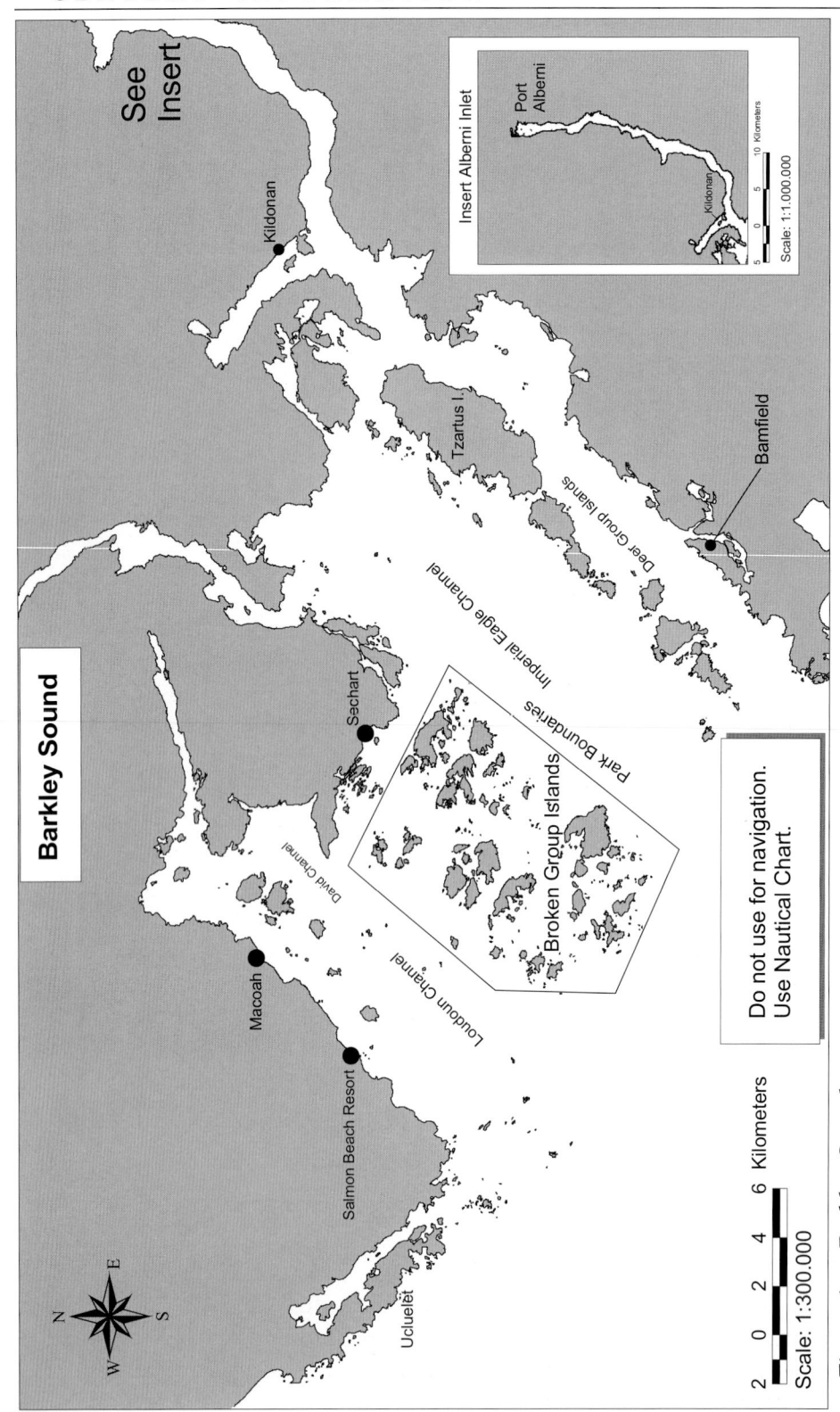

Figure 1 – Barkley Sound

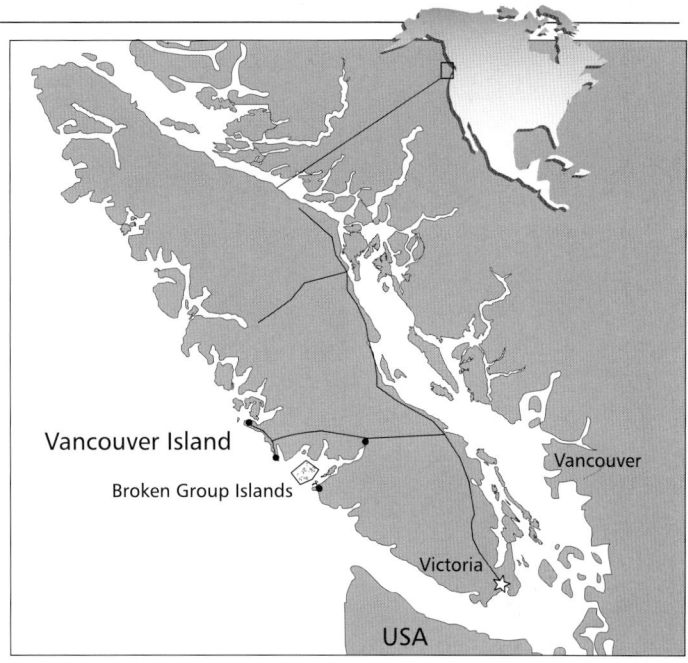

Figure 2
Vancouver Island

BARKLEY SOUND

Vancouver Island is approximately 450 km long and 100 km wide. The Vancouver Island mountain range, with peaks above 1,000 m, runs lengthwise down the centre of the island. Barkley Sound is situated on the west coast of Vancouver Island. It is an 800 sq km, rectangular bay bordered by large channels and inlets. The city of Port Alberni is located at the end of the longest, Alberni Inlet. The village of Ucluelet is situated on the northwest side of Barkley Sound, and Bamfield lies 30 km across the sound to the southeast. Toquart Bay and Alberni Inlet border Barkley Sound to the north while the Amphitrite Point and Cape Beale lighthouses are the southern borders. Barkley Sound is comprised of three major groups of islands: the Deer Group, the Pinkerton Group and the Broken Group. The sound, along with the outer coast of south Vancouver Island, has been nicknamed "Graveyard of the Pacific" because of the countless ships that have met their demise on its reefs and rocky shores.

Captain Charles Barkley, a 25-year-old fur trader, was the first European to explore the sound that now bears his name. Barkley was captain of the British trading vessel *Imperial Eagle,* and arrived on the west coast in 1787 with his 17-year-old wife, Frances Hornby Trevor Barkley. He anchored in Effingham Bay during his first visit to the BGI.

Europeans did not settle the rugged west coast after Barkley's explorations because the land was unsuitable for subsistence farming. Most of the islands in Barkley Sound were named by Captain George Henry Richards during his survey of the area in 1861.

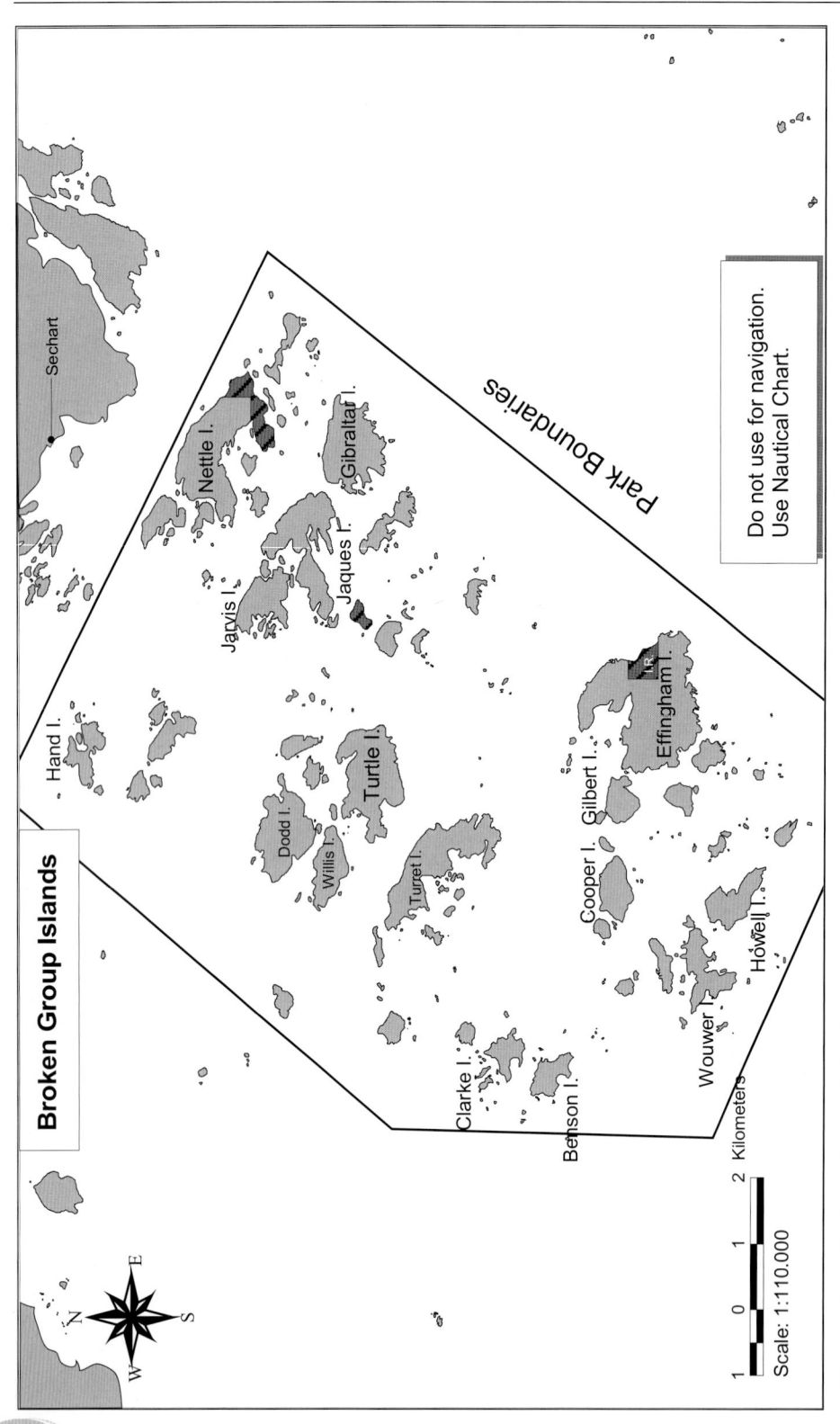

Figure 3 – Broken Group Islands

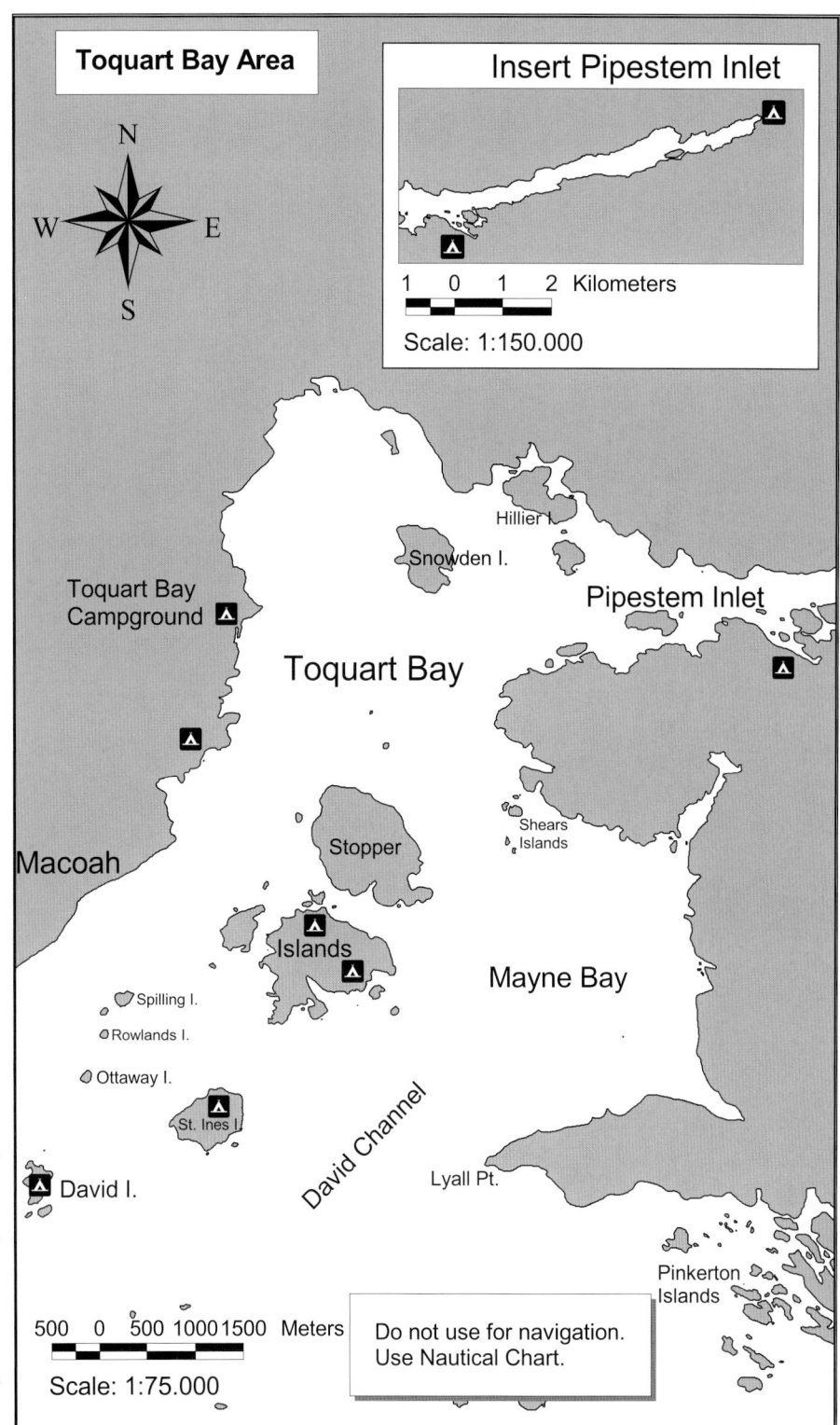

Toquart Bay Area

Insert Pipestem Inlet

1 0 1 2 Kilometers

Scale: 1:150.000

N
W E
S

Hillier I.
Snowden I.

Toquart Bay
Campground

Pipestem Inlet

Toquart Bay

Macoah

Stopper

Shears
Islands

Islands

Mayne Bay

Spilling I.
Rowlands I.
Ottaway I.
St. Ines I.
David I.

David Channel

Lyall Pt.

Pinkerton
Islands

500 0 500 1000 1500 Meters

Do not use for navigation.
Use Nautical Chart.

Scale: 1:75.000

Figure 4 – Toquart Bay Area

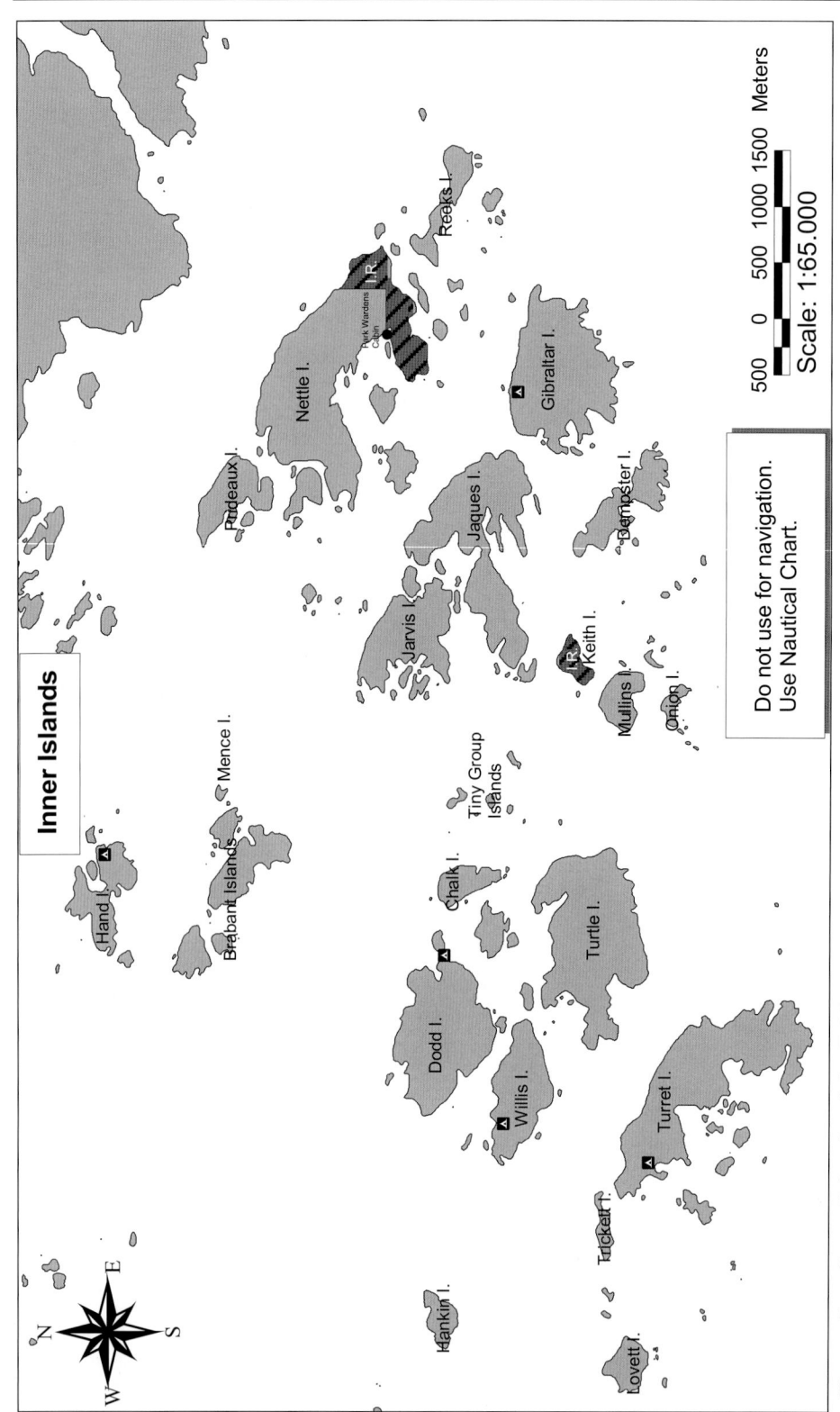

Figure 5 – Inner Islands of the BGI

Figure 6 – Outer Islands of the BGI

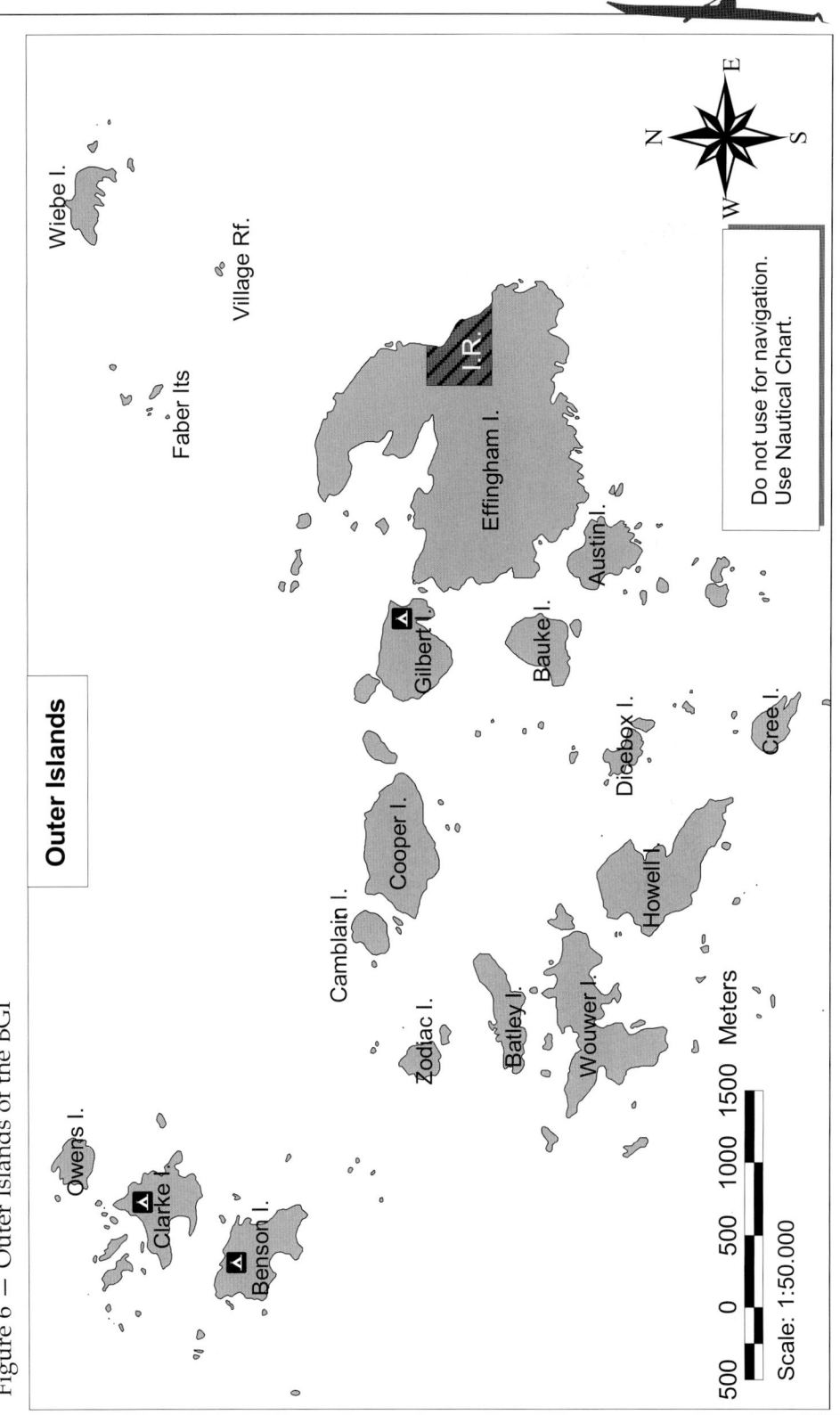

Outer Islands

Do not use for navigation.
Use Nautical Chart.

Scale: 1:50.000

500   0   500   1000   1500   Meters

These glass balls drifted from Japan. Glass balls are beachcombers' favourite treasures. Photo: Wendy Szaniszlo

PACIFIC RIM NATIONAL PARK RESERVE

In 1970 the Canadian federal government established Pacific Rim National Park Reserve (PRNPR) in order to protect a representative sample of the coastal mountains and the west coast Vancouver Island marine regions. The park encompasses an area of 49,962 hectares, 43% of which is marine. PRNPR was officially gazetted in 2001, though it remains a national park "reserve" because it includes land involved in pending First Nations land claims.

PRNPR consists of three units, each created in a different year: the Long Beach unit, between Ucluelet and Tofino (created in 1971); the Broken Groups Islands, in Barkley Sound (created in 1973); and the West Coast Trail, the former lifesaving trail stretching between Bamfield and Port Renfrew (created in 1975).

Though designated as a protected area, the land and ecology of PRNPR endures a myriad of stresses brought about by almost one million visitors per year (mostly to the Long Beach unit), as well as adjacent Indian Reserves, an airport, and the commercial fishing and logging activities that abut its border.

Long Beach is the most accessible and most visited of the Park's three units. Its spectacular sandy beaches stretch for over 30 km of beautiful coastline. Surfing is a popular activity and many locals hit the surf with almost religious

zeal. Surfing is an important part of the local culture. During the winter, Long Beach offers first-rate opportunities for storm watching.

The world famous West Coast Trail stretches 77 km along the rugged open coast south of Bamfield. More than 50 ships have been wrecked along this part of the coast; the remains of some can still be seen (MacFarlane *et al.* 1996:7). In 1906, the steamer *Valencia* ran aground in this area in a storm and 136 people lost their lives. Public outcry over this tragedy spurred the government into constructing a lifesaving trail along the coastline to facilitate rescues. A cabin was built every six miles and stocked with provisions for survivors of shipwrecks.

As new technologies for navigation and marine safety were developed, the lifesaving trail gradually became obsolete. Eventually it was designated the West Coast Trail, one of Canada's premier recreational backpacking trails. The West Coast Trail is open from May 1 to September 30.

The Broken Group Islands (BGI) unit of PRNPR is approximately 106 sq km, most of which is water. This archipelago is a well-known paradise for kayakers and outdoor enthusiasts pursuing a wilderness experience. It also offers a great destination for sailboats and marine vessels to explore and anchor in the sheltered waters. SCUBA diving is popular, particularly in winter when the water visibility is better.

View of the western outer islands, BGI. Photo: Wendy Szaniszlo

Toquart Bay, Barkley Sound. Photo: Barbara Schramm

ACCESS TO THE BROKEN GROUP ISLANDS

There are several settlements on the shores of Barkley Sound from which kayakers can access the Broken Group Islands — Ucluelet, Bamfield, Sechart (via a scenic cruise on the M.V. *Frances Barkley*), and Toquart Bay (the most popular). The route to all these places normally leads through Port Alberni.

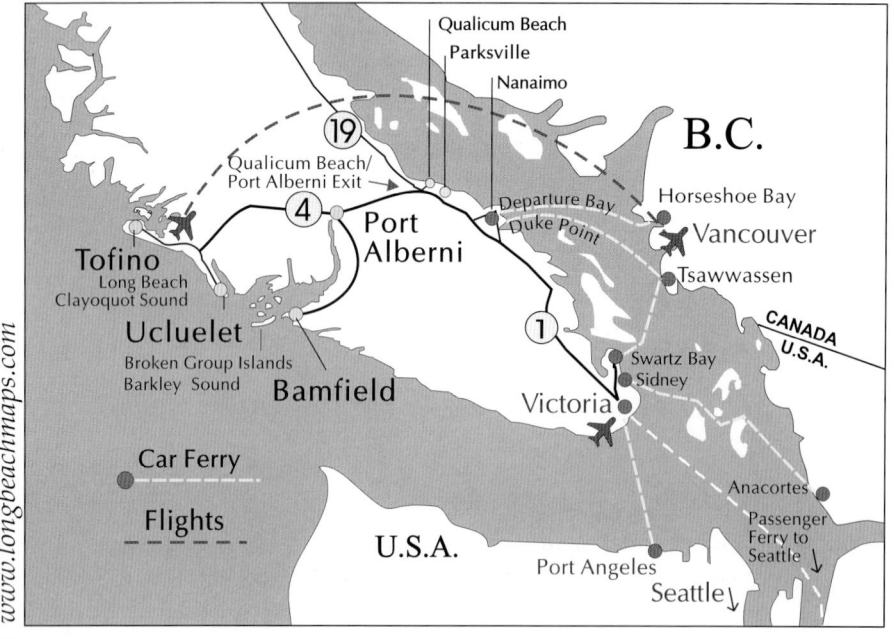

Figure 7 — Road map

PORT ALBERNI

Port Alberni is a forestry-based town with a population of about 18,000. The city was named after Spanish Lieutenant Colonel Don Pedro de Alberni, who was posted at Nootka Sound and never actually visited the Port Alberni area. In 1964 an 8-m tidal wave triggered by an earthquake in Alaska caused considerable damage in the town. Incredibly, no lives were lost. The Pacific Rim area is geologically very active, though, luckily, tsunamis are rare.

Welcoming figures, Port Alberni

Port Alberni is well supplied with grocery stores, restaurants, a hospital, hotels and motels, and major stores where kayakers can top up their supplies, stop for a meal, stay overnight or, with luck, replace any forgotten items.

To get to Port Alberni from Nanaimo, drive north on Highway 19 (the Island Highway). Take the exit for Qualicum Beach and Port Alberni onto Highway 4, and follow the signs to Port Alberni. The routes to

Alberni Inlet. Photos: B. Schramm

Bamfield, Ucluelet and Toquart Bay split off from there. The *Frances Barkley* can be boarded at Harbour Quay, on the Port Alberni waterfront. More detailed directions follow.

Kayak Rental in Port Alberni:
Alberni Outpost: www.albernioutpost.com 1-800-325-3921

Ucluelet Harbour in morning mist. Photo: Barbara Schramm

UCLUELET

The village of Ucluelet ("yoo-*clue*-let") is situated on a peninsula at the outer, northern corner of Barkley Sound. Its name comes from the local First Nation's language and means "place with a safe harbour." The first settlers in Ucluelet were sealers, who arrived in the late 1800s. World War II boosted the town's development with construction of a seaplane military base, new infrastructure and a road connecting Ucluelet with Tofino's military airport. The road to Port Alberni was built in 1959. Before being paved in 1972, the 110-km-long road was very rough. Despite improvements over subsequent decades, the winding route is still a challenge to drive, particularly during darkness, heavy rain or fog. Close to one million people visit Ucluelet, Tofino and the Long Beach unit of PRNPR each year. Traffic volume can be high, especially during the summer and on holiday weekends.

Until recently, Ucluelet's economy was based on natural resources, mainly mining, logging and fishing. Logging and fishing are still important, despite a decline over the last decade. Ucluelet used to have nine fish plants, but now only a few remain operational. Tourism is currently booming and provides employment and income to the village's 1,500 residents. Outdoor recreational opportunities abound in Ucluelet, including sportfishing, whale watching, surfing, nature cruises, mountain biking, nature interpretation tours, wildlife viewing, hiking, kayaking and beachcombing.

Ucluelet is 100 km from Port Alberni, a drive that normally takes 1.5 h but can take two or more if there is heavy traffic or road work (not uncommon during summer months). Keep to the right fork as you are coming into Port Alberni. It turns into Johnson St., which continues downhill to the water, and then take a right turn along the river to follow Highway 4 out

Amphitrite lighthouse in Ucluelet. Photo: Barbara Schramm

of town. The route is well marked because of the large number of visitors who head to Tofino (population: 1600 people) and Ucluelet.

Ucluelet has a medical clinic and ambulance service. The area hospital is located 42 km away in Tofino. The so-called Tofino Coast Guard Radio is located on Amphitrite Point in Ucluelet (apparently foreign mariners found "Ucluelet" difficult to pronounce), along with the Coast Guard's Vessel Traffic Management service, marine traffic controller for the considerable number of commercial ships entering and exiting Juan de Fuca Strait. A Coast Guard Auxiliary branch conducts search-and-rescue operations in the waters near Ucluelet.

The Coast Guard maintains a radar station that looks like a gigantic golf ball atop Mount Ozzard (792 m elevation), across the harbour from Ucluelet. The views of Ucluelet and Barkley and Clayoquot Sounds from Mount Ozzard are spectacular on a clear day. On clear nights the light of Amphitrite Point lighthouse can be seen from the BGI.

Amphitrite Point is 13 km from Benson Island in the BGI. This crossing can be very dangerous and is only suitable for advanced kayakers[1]. Crossing time depends on where you launch in Ucluelet, and is strongly influenced by wind and weather conditions. The best time to attempt the crossing is during the early morning, when wind and waves are generally more benign.

---

[1] An advanced kayaker can be defined as one who can consistently roll and self-rescue in rough sea. They can paddle with confidence in winds up to 20 knots, currents up to 4 knots, wind waves up to 1 m, swells to 3 m, and surf to 1.5 m.

Gray whale feeding in Barkley Sound. Photo: Wendy Szaniszlo

Expect boat traffic during the summer; keep your group close together and make sure you can be detected during fog if you don't want to become a speed bump!

During this crossing, gray whales can frequently be seen near Chrow Island, Sykes Reef, Starlight Reef, Mara Rock, Great Bear Rock and Alley Rock. A sea otter, affectionately known as Olley by the local nature tour operators, is frequently seen at Alley Rock.

Water taxis for kayakers from Ucluelet:

> Subtidal Adventures: www.subtidaladventures.com   1-877-444-1134
> Bostrom Charters: www.oceankayaking.com   (250) 726-8166
> Beachcomber Ocean Tours: www.wildedgewhales.com   1-877-363-22

Kayak Rental in Ucluelet:

> Coastal Knights: www.coastalknights.com   (250) 726-4202
> Majestic Ocean Kayaking: www.oceankayaking.com   1-800-889-7644

Bamfiled Marine Sciences Centre
Photo:B. Schramm

BAMFIELD

Thirty km across Barkley Sound from Ucluelet sits Bamfield, a tiny, quaint fishing village where everybody knows everybody. Bamfield was named (with a slight shift in spelling) after William Eddy Banfield, the first settler in Barkley Sound, who arrived in 1859. Banfield was also a government agent and a trader. The village of Bamfield has a Coast Guard station and is also home to the Bamfield Marine Station. This facility was formerly the Bamfield cable station, erected in 1902 as the terminus of the trans-Pacific telegraph line to Australia — an important part of the British Empire's global cable network.

Bamfield is about 90 km from Port Alberni, a 2 h drive on a well maintained logging road. Follow the signs from Port Alberni. Drive with your lights on, watch for potholes and yield to logging trucks. Bamfield can also be reached from Victoria via Duncan, Lake Cowichan and about 120 km of logging road.

Bamfield is approximately 15 km from the campsite on Gibraltar Island in the BGI. This crossing can be very dangerous and is for advanced kayakers only. The recommended time to attempt it is during the early morning hours when sea conditions are calmer. Expect boat traffic in Trevor Channel during the summer and make sure you are visible during fog. Trevor and Imperial Eagle channels can be very challenging for paddlers. Between the channels is the Deer Group archipelago, a great place for kayaking despite the limited places to camp.

Broken Islands Adventures, based in Bamfield, rents kayaks and offers nature cruises and water taxi services to Barkley Sound.

Broken Island Adventures
1-888-728-6200
www.brokenislandadventures.com

Whale skeletons at Sechart in 1906.
Copyright BC Archives D–03824

Sechart Whaling Station at the turn of
the century. Copyright Parks Canada

SECHART

Sechart has a fascinating history. Its name is derived from the Tseshaht First Nation, who maintained a summer village nearby. In 1905, commercial whaling began on the west coast when the Pacific Whaling Company, of Victoria, built a whaling station at Sechart (Peterson, 1999:112). Whales, mainly humpbacks, were hunted for their meat, oil and bones, which were rich in phosphate and used as fertilizer or animal feed.

Heavy whaling activity created intense pressure on the regional whale populations, resulting in a dramatic drop in the number of whales (see tables below). Profitability declined, and the last year the Pacific Whaling Company operated out of Sechart was 1917. Old harpoon heads can still occasionally be uncovered at low tide or when SCUBA diving in the area.

In 1926, the whaling station was turned into a fish reduction plant, where fish meal and oil were manufactured from pilchard and dogfish until the late 1930s (Peterson, 1999:119).

**Whales processed per year at
Sechart Whaling Station
(1908–1917)**

Source: (Peterson, 1999:113)

Year	Number
1908	250
1909	359
1910	427
1911	474
1912	284
1913	274
1914	86
1917	90
Total	2244

Species of whale processed at Sechart Whaling Station (1908–1917)

Species	Number	Percentage
Blue	109	4.9 %
Bluenose	1	0.05 %
Fin	220	9.8 %
Grey	1	0.05 %
Humpback	1869	83.3%
Sei	29	1.3%
Sperm	15	0.6 %
Total	2244	100%

Source: (Peterson, 1999:113)

In 1995 the former administrative building of forestry company MacMillan Bloedel was moved by barge — all 203 tons of it — 65 km from Port Alberni to Sechart, where it is now a year-round lodge for visitors, kayakers and forestry workers. Sechart offers home-cooked meals, hot showers, canoe and kayak rental, and water taxi services. There is no road access to Sechart Lodge. The only access is by water via kayak, water taxi or the coastal freighter M.V. *Frances Barkley*.

A blue whale being processed. Copyright British Columbia Archives A–09217

M.V. Lady Rose at the former dock near Gibraltar Island. Copyright Parks Canada

Lady Rose Marine Services, based at Harbour Quay in Port Alberni, owns and operates Sechart Lodge, along with the coastal freighters M.V. *Lady Rose* and M.V. *Frances Barkley*. These two vessels annually transport 15,000 passengers, along with tons of freight, groceries, supplies and mail, to the villages, cabins and fishing and logging camps located in and around Barkley Sound. The two vessels can easily be recognized by their size and their black hulls and white decks.

The *Lady Rose* was built in Scotland in 1937 and was the first diesel-powered, single propeller vessel to cross the Atlantic Ocean. This well-known west coast vessel is 32 m long, with a beam of 6.7 m. She can carry up to 100 passengers and 25 tons of cargo. From 1942 to 1946, before there was a road between Port Alberni and Ucluelet, the vessel was used by the Royal Canadian Army Service Corps to carry army personnel, cargo, food and mail. In 1960 the *Lady Rose* was put back into service in Barkley Sound as a vital transportation link.

In 1990, Lady Rose Marine Services purchased a ferry in Norway. It arrived in Port Alberni after a journey of 51 days and was renamed M.V. *Frances Barkley*, in honour of Captain Charles Barkley's wife. The *Frances Barkley*, with a length of 39 m and beam of 7.3 m, can carry up to 200 passengers and 100 tons of cargo.

From June through the third week of September each year, the *Frances Barkley* services the Broken Group Islands on a regular basis. Passengers board the ship in Port Alberni and cruise down picturesque Alberni Inlet, a large fjord surrounded by mountains. Many salmon streams drain into the inlet, and bears can often be seen at low tide. You can also buy a quick meal on board.

Kayakers are dropped off in Sechart after a cruise of about three hours. (Until 1991 kayakers could ask to be dropped at a floating dock near Gibraltar Island, but this has been discontinued.) Once in Sechart, Parks Canada wardens give an orientation to visitors prior to their trip into the BGI. The best way for beginner paddlers to access the BGI is from Sechart.

Reserving space for your group (along with gear and kayaks) is strongly suggested. Contact:

> Lady Rose Marine Services
> 5425 Argyle Street, Port Alberni, BC V9Y 1T6
> (250) 723-8313 or toll-free 1-800-663-7192 Water taxi: (250) 720-7358
> www.ladyrosemarine.com

M.V. Frances Barkley docked at Sechart Whaling Station. Photo: JF Marleau

TOQUART BAY

Toquart Bay was a trading post in the 1860s, a cannery in the 1960s, and a mining centre in the late 1960s. The Brynnor mine, operated by Noranda, was located several km inland from Toquart Bay on the Toquart Bay Road. Large ships docked at Toquart Bay to load iron ore for shipment to Japan. Remains of the dock can still be seen. During its seven years of operation (between 1963 and 1969), approximately two hundred people were employed by the mine and five million tons of ore were exported. The open pit mine is 21 acres in size, 400 m deep and is now filled with water. It can be seen on the right-hand side of Toquart Bay Road just before Maggie Lake, when driving toward the campground. Old machinery still lies at the bottom of this artificially-formed lake.

Toquart Bay is one of the main access points to the BGI. To get there, drive through Port Alberni following the directions to Ucluelet and Tofino. Toward the outskirts of Port Alberni you will find a Petro-Canada gas station. Note your odometer reading there. The Toquart Bay Road turnoff is 78 km after the gas station, on the left-hand side of the highway.

Toquart Bay Road is a logging road and drivers should always stay on the main route. Drive with your headlights on; watch for logging trucks and yield when you meet one. The road is rough and only suitable for vehicles with a high clearance. The first 400 m are steep and rugged, but the rest is relatively better. Road conditions can become very bad due to heavy precipitation and lack of maintenance.

The Toquart Bay kayak launch is located at the Forest Recreation Site, which is managed by the Toquaht First Nation. The site has a long sandy beach, boat launch, parking lots, picnic tables, toilets, and RV and tent sites. The beach at Toquart Bay is almost entirely composed of fine tailings from the concentrator of the now defunct Brynnor mine. The Toquaht First Nation is currently planning to develop the marina and built more infrastructure. Toquart Bay is popular with sport fishers during the summer months, and is crowded during July and August.

When paddling from Toquart Bay toward the BGI, David Channel (between Hand Island and the Stopper Islands) can be very challenging. Crossing David Channel in the morning or evening, when winds are lighter, is recommended.

Toquart Bay Campground
www.toquartbay.com
(250) 726-8349

Solar composting toilets at campsites. Copyright JF Marleau

Campsites and low-impact practices

T he Broken Group Islands is a place of incredible natural beauty. However, this small area undergoes a lot of stress during the summer months. The ecological integrity of this archipelago could be compromised if visitors don't take responsibility for minimizing their ecological impact. Let future visitors enjoy a great wilderness experience too! Practicing low-impact camping is vital to preserving the wilderness.

Note that "mothershipping," which refers to kayakers sleeping on board a larger vessel and doing kayak day-trips from the "mother ship," is prohibited in the BGI by Parks Canada regulation. This means paddlers must camp on the islands and be completely self-sufficient. Other Parks Canada policies and regulations apply in the BGI. For example, except for park management purposes or as permitted by business license, it is prohibited to land any power vessel at a BGI campsite in order to pick up or drop off people, provisions or equipment. For more information call PRNPR at (250) 726-7721.

GENERAL INFORMATION

Consider all fresh water sources in the BGI as unfit for drinking. Animal fecal coliform contamination is always a threat. In the summer, creeks on the islands are dry or almost dry. It is strongly recommended that you bring enough water for your entire trip. Plan on consuming three litres per day per person. Water can be obtained at Sechart Lodge.

The upside of the water shortage is that mosquitoes, which need fresh water for reproduction, are usually only annoying during the spring. Only females bite and they are attracted by the carbon dioxide (CO_2) we exhale.

After a day of paddling and exploration, campsites are places to meet other paddlers and share stories around a fire. If you expect to have an entire campsite exclusively for your group, you should probably stay home or paddle elsewhere.

The islands of the BGI are distributed in clusters, and most clusters include a campsite. Though the BGI includes over 100 islands and islets, you are only allowed to camp at eight designated campsites, located on Hand, Dodd, Willis, Turret, Gibraltar, Clarke, Benson and Gilbert Islands. Most of these are former First Nations villages or camps. Each campsite is equipped with solar composting toilets, but none has a reliable source of fresh water. **It is illegal to camp anywhere in the BGI other than at designated campsites.** This regulation is intended to reduce environmental impact, and is strictly enforced by the Park wardens.

July through to the Labour Day weekend (first weekend in September) is considered peak season. Even though overnight use in the BGI has decreased since 2003, you should be prepared to share your campsite with other visitors, especially during peak season. (The exception is Benson Island, which generally sees fewer visitors.) Dodd and Willis, the more popular sites, can have up to 50 campers each per night during peak season. Commercial groups prefer these two islands because their ideal location allows groups to set up base camp and make several day trips. Large groups are relatively slow to pack up and move camp, and guided groups avoid moving their campsites too frequently. Small groups of recreational kayakers, on the other hand, are usually quicker to move on.

Visitors can change campsite or maintain a base camp as long as their stay does not exceed four nights at the same campsite. The maximum stay in the BGI is 14 days. From May 1 to the end of September, fee collectors based at Sechart visit each campsite to collect Park user fees and issue camping permits. At the time of this writing, the user fee is $9.90 CDN per person per night. Fees can be paid with cash or credit card.

Please avoid leaving any trace of your stay, including fire pits.
Photo: JF Marleau

THE BROKEN WINDOW THEORY

Researchers in the United States have developed a "Broken Window" theory, which explains the gradual degradation of a neighbourhood. It happens like this: A window gets broken in an apartment building, but no one fixes it. Later, another window is broken; again it is left unfixed. Then graffiti starts to appear, along with other damage. Soon destruction and neglect increase exponentially. The building depreciates and tenants move out. Crime moves in and the situation worsens. The Broken Window theory says that visible evidence of abuse or decay invites more abuse or decay.

Here's another illustration of the theory, in a more familiar situation. Imagine you go to dinner at a new friend's house. You use the washroom and are impressed with its cleanliness. You feel compelled to leave the washroom as clean and tidy as you found it. If the washroom is dirty and messy, however, you will be less likely to care about wiping up the water you've dripped on the counter or straightening the hand towel after you use it.

The Broken Window theory is also applicable to the BGI. If people neglect the campsites by leaving even a little bit of garbage or other visual signs of disturbance, others will be more likely do the same because of the lack of informal social pressure. During your trip, as your food supply is consumed and your storage space increases, please set an example by picking up litter left by other campers.

LOW-IMPACT ACTIVITY GUIDELINES FOR THE BROKEN GROUP ISLANDS

The following low-impact guidelines were developed by Pacific Rim National Park Reserve through consultations with kayak operators. These guidelines are conditions of use for all commercial kayak businesses licensed to operate within PRNPR. Items in **boldface** are a Canada National Park Regulation and/or Superintendent Notice and must be followed by all visitors to the BGI. Most other items must be followed by commercial kayak businesses operating in the park. Recreational kayakers are also strongly encouraged to follow these guidelines. Note that the guidelines listed below are a summary adapted from the original version.

Low impact camping.
Photo: JF Marleau

CAMPING

- **Camping is prohibited without a permit.** Attendants will visit the eight designated campsites daily to gather fees and issue permits.

- **Camp only in the designated campsite areas located on the following eight islands: Hand, Gibraltar, Dodd, Willis, Turret, Gilbert, Clark and Benson.**

- **Maximum group size in the BGI is ten people.**
- **Neither private nor guided groups may reserve a campsite.**
- Keep groups small and contained in one area.
- Leave campsites as clean as or cleaner than when you arrived.
- Dismantle any structures that you have built before moving camp.
- Avoid critical wildlife habitats, obvious animal trails and fragile terrain.
- Do not cut trees or vegetation.
- Do not drive nails into trees.
- Do not trench around tents. Choose well-drained or high ground instead.
- Watch where you walk; use established trails to avoid trampling vegetation.

FIRES

- **Beach fires are permitted in designated campsites.**
- **Fires must be a safe distance from drift logs.**
- **Fires are prohibited under or near the tree canopy or in sandy areas with evidence of large root systems underneath.**

- Fires must be small enough to put out quickly and completely.
- Fuel must consist only of driftwood found on beaches below the high-tide line, and must be small enough to burn down completely to ashes. It is illegal to collect wood in the forest or to cut any tree, even a dead one.
- Once a fire has been extinguished, all signs of the fire must be obliterated.
- Temporary fire bans are strictly enforced.
- Make your fire below the high-tide line.
- Portable stoves should always be carried for preparing meals.
- Restrict fires to the size of your kayak's cargo hatch.
- Watch the wind direction to make sure flying sparks won't burn holes in your tarp or tent.
- Take only what you need. Driftwood can become rare during the summer months, especially on the more frequented islands.
- Burn only driftwood no larger in diameter than your fist. Make sure it is light; heavy driftwood holds too much water and won't burn well.
- Crush any charcoal, then remove all charred remains by scattering in the ocean.
- Do not construct a ring of rocks around fires; this scars the rocks and disturbs habitat. Heated rocks can explode and become a safety hazard.
- Dismantle any fire pits you may find.

ETIQUETTE

- Collecting natural objects (such as seashells, feathers, bones, etc.) is prohibited in national parks.
- Do not paddle into sea caves.
- Dogs are not permitted in the BGI.
- Unless safety is compromised, have only one group per company at each campsite.
- It is unlawful to feed wildlife in a national park.
- Keep noise levels at a minimum at campsites, on trails and on the water.
- Store gear neatly when on shore. Keep a tidy campsite.
- Cooperate and communicate in a friendly manner with other groups.
- A voluntary no-angling, no-harvesting policy applies.

Wolves on Howell Island. Photo: Jillian Brown

WILDLIFE

- Be aware and knowledgeable of sensitive sites (breeding areas, nesting sites, sea lion haulouts, etc.) and do not approach these sites so disturbance is minimized.

- Stay a minimum distance of 100 m from wildlife. Back away at the first sign of disturbance.

- When in the proximity of wildlife, conduct yourself in a manner that does not disturb or alter its natural behavior (without compromising the safety of your group). Persistent and recurring disturbance by people interrupts the animals' ability to rest, feed, court and tend young, and causes them to expend more energy than they otherwise would. However, it is very important to teach wolves and bears that it is not acceptable to approach you or your campsite by shouting, banging pots, waving, etc. to scare them off.

- Use binoculars and telephoto lenses, rather than close approach, to observe and photograph wildlife.

- Store food securely inside kayak hatches, except when park wardens have issued a (rare) bear warning for the BGI.

- Keep other kayakers informed about sites where people and wildlife have had problems with each other. Any incidents should be reported to park wardens.

- Select kayak launch sites carefully to avoid trampling intertidal life.

- Tread carefully when exploring the intertidal zone, and return all rocks, shells, and creatures to their original location.

HUMAN WASTE

- Use solar privies wherever they are provided. Each campsite has solar powered composting toilets.
- Plan to stop at designated sites where solar privies are located.
- Antibacterial products prevent solar privies from functioning. All products with antibacterial agents (i.e. sani-wipes) must be packed out.
- If no solar composting toilet is available, use the intertidal zone. Find a secluded place on a beach, away from campsites and at least 100 m from running water. Dig a shallow hole about 15 cm deep in the sand and cover it after use. Try washing off with salt water as an alternative to toilet paper; otherwise all toilet paper must be burned or packed out. Carry Ziploc bags for used toilet paper.
- All feminine hygiene products must be packed out.

WASTE WATER

- Use biodegradable soap.
- Drain waste water from cooking into the ocean.
- Wash dishes at the ocean's edge or dump waste water into the ocean at water's edge.
- Brush teeth at the ocean's edge and spit into the water.

WASTE

- **Do not put garbage or food scraps in privies.**
- Reduce the amount of potential garbage. Plan your meal quantities carefully, package food in reusable containers and use leftovers for snacks or lunches.
- Food waste must be packed out, or completely burned where appropriate.
- As your kayaks become emptier, begin to fill them up with litter from the beaches that you can bring back with you and recycle.

FIRST NATIONS

- **You must have a current letter of permission from the Tseshaht First Nation to enter Indian reserves on Nettle, Effingham and Keith Islands.**
- **Do not remove or handle cultural objects.**
- **Do not enter burial caves.**
- Do not walk on fish traps.

Hope for the best, be ready for the worst. Photo: Wendy Szaniszlo

Safety

Kayakers in the BGI have an array of different attitudes, judgement, knowledge, skills and experience. Often, beginner kayakers don't know what they don't know. Frequently, for example, beginner kayakers from landlocked areas have no clue what a tide is. Knowing the tides is especially important for choosing a tent site and deciding where to safely park your kayak for the night. Sometimes kayaks "mysteriously" disappear in the BGI, stolen by the tide due to the negligence of their owners. Parks officials generally assume the worst if an empty kayak is found drifting on the tide, and will immediately launch a large-scale search operation. Such a search is costly and puts those involved at risk. Make sure you are not responsible for initiating a search for an improperly managed kayak!

Common sense is critical for your own safety. If unsure, err on the side of caution. Hope for the best but be prepared for the worst. Always be conservative when planning your route — there's no need to rush. Slow down and enjoy each minute in this paradise! Consider the skills and abilities of all group members in order to facilitate an enjoyable, comfortable and safe trip.

Always bring extra clothes, food and water in case your schedule is delayed due to bad weather. Even on a day trip, pack for an emergency overnight stay. It is particularly important to pack sufficient water. The most frequent

illness during a kayak trip is dehydration. Don't wait to get a dehydration headache before drinking some water.

Make sure you always store your food and dishes safely because they can attract rodents such as deer mice. A large percentage of deer mice population carry the hantavirus. This disease is spread through mice droppings and in extreme cases can be fatal to humans.

SKILLS

Sea kayaking involves a wide variety of different skills, some directly to do with the paddling of the vessel, some with keeping track of where you are going, and others which involve coping with the marine environment, which can change rapidly. It is not in the scope of this book to teach these skills, beyond mentioning what you should know before venturing into the west coast waters.

You should not embark on your trip in the BGI without a cell phone, VHF radio, or preferably both. You should also have a marine chart, a compass or GPS, and the knowledge to use these tools. The myriad islands in the Broken Group can be challenging to navigate. Every year people get lost due to poor navigation skills,

Do not forget a communication device and a GPS or compass.

particularly in the fog. A mistake could have you heading toward Japan, paddling into danger or, at minimum, going in circles. Learn how to use your brand new compass and fancy GPS. Do you know what the symbols mean on the marine chart? How far is a nautical mile? How many miles do you paddle in an hour? What does declination mean? Can you find your way back to your campsite if fog rolls in unexpectedly?

I strongly recommend that you know and practice self-rescues and assisted rescues. What would you do if you or a member of your group capsized in rough seas? Have you practiced? How long does it take you to do a self-rescue? If you don't know how to do rescues, it is probably time to learn from professional, certified instructors. If you have any questions regarding which company will meet your kayak training needs, expectations and budget, don't hesitate to contact Pacific Rim Informative Adventures at info@priaoutback.com.

WINTER PADDLING

Paddling in the BGI in winter is permitted, but not recommended. Park wardens are stationed in the islands only from the beginning of May to the end of October. Conditions can become very dangerous during the winter (November through March), with frequent storms, high winds and large swell. Paddling during the winter months is for advanced or expert kayakers. For safety, beginner and intermediate paddlers should have a certified lead guide with them.

Despite the storms, relentless pouring rain and short daylight hours, winter paddling in the BGI offers a unique wilderness experience. With the solitude, abundant wildlife and great visibility in very clear water, you can really feel at one with nature. It doesn't storm every day during the winter — there *are* sunny periods. It's possible to pick a day of good weather and do day trips in the islands from Sechart, or arrange a shuttle from Ucluelet. But always exercise extreme caution when paddling on the west coast in winter. April and October usually offer decent weather and are good shoulder-season months for kayaking.

CANADIAN COAST GUARD REGULATIONS

Kayaks in Canadian waters must meet Canadian Coast Guard regulations. Each kayaker must carry:

- a Personal Flotation Device (PFD) all time when on the water
- a pump or bailing device
- a spare paddle
- a whistle
- navigation lights, if travelling after dark (a normal headlamp is sufficient for a kayak)
- 15 metres of buoyant heaving line

IN CASE OF EMERGENCY
OR TO REPORT VIOLATIONS

Park wardens provide information to visitors, enforce national park laws and regulations, protect natural resources, conduct search-and-rescue operations, and provide first aid. In case of emergency, park wardens are your first line of help. They are professionally trained and have legal jurisdiction in national parks. Do not hesitate to report any violations or suspicious activity to them. During the summer months, park wardens are very busy. Your eyes and ears are important and your reported observations are very much appreciated.

Parks Canada warden. Photo: Barbara Schramm

Park wardens are stationed in the BGI from May through October at a floating cabin on the east side of Nettle Island. They can be reached by cell phone at 250-726-8175 or by VHF radio on channel 16 via call sign "Broken Group Warden." Every kayak group should have a cell phone or VHF radio — it is strongly recommended to carry both. Cell phones work relatively well in the Broken Group Islands and the northwest part of Barkley Sound, especially those using Canadian cell phone companies such Telus or Rogers. If you have difficulty getting reception, try moving to a position in line-of-sight with Mount Ozzard (the mountain near Ucluelet with the "golf ball" radar station).

CONTACT NUMBERS

Broken Group Wardens: 250-726-8175 (cell) or VHF channel 16 (call sign "Broken Group Warden")

Canadian Coast Guard: 1-800-567-5111 or *16 (cell) or VHF channel 16 (call sign "Tofino Coast Guard Radio")

Ucluelet RCMP: 250-726-7773

Ucluelet Medical Clinic: 250-726-4443

Tofino General Hospital: 250-725-3212

Rescue Coordination Centre: 1-800-567-5111 or *311(cell)

GUIDED TOURS

Some kayakers prefer to use the services of a commercial kayak outfitter for their expedition to ensure their safety, to enjoy gourmet meals, and to learn more about the local natural and cultural history. If you are doing an expedition with a kayak outfitter, make sure the company's guides are certified. All kayak guides legally operating in the BGI must be certified with organizations such as the Sea Kayak Guides Alliance of British Columbia (SKGABC), the Canadian Federation of Ocean Kayak Educators (CFOKE), or the Association of Canadian Sea Kayak Guides (ACSKG). All companies operating in the BGI must have a valid business licence. Prior to the start of overnight trips, guides must contact park wardens by phone and provide the following information: name of company, guide's name, number of guests, guest health issues and expected campsite location. Park wardens in turn provide current information such as closures, wildlife observations or issues, campsite status reports, and other pertinent information.

British Columbia has the highest training and safety standards for sea kayak guides in the world. Pacific Rim National Park Reserve endorses, promotes, and enforces these standards. Before the standards were in effect anybody could call themselves a guide, whether or not they knew how to use a compass or perform rescues. Unfortunately, some companies still prefer to hire low-wage, non-certified guides with skills and knowledge inadequate to ensure guest safety.

Kayak companies must also respect guide-to-client ratios. These ratios are one certified lead guide for five guests, or one certified lead guide and one certified assistant guide for up to eight guests. These standards ensure a high level of safety and enjoyment for national park visitors. If you are dealing with a "pirate" company that has uncertified lead guides and oversized groups, your group will be in jeopardy of being warned, fined, or possibly evicted from the BGI. Pirate companies often fail to meet the requirements for liability insurance as well.

Persons interested in going on a guided kayak trip generally have two main concerns: a good price and a great destination. It is very important to check on the reputation of the company, the quality of their equipment, the transportation, accommodation and meals provided, and the guides' certification. Pacific Rim Informative Adventures (PRIA) offers kayak training courses and certified guide services to several kayak outfitters operating in the BGI. If you have any questions regarding which company will meet your kayaking needs, expectations and budget, don't hesitate to contact PRIA at info@priaoutback.com.

Weather conditions can change quickly from sun to fog or wind driven waves.
Photo: Barbara Schramm

Weather

Barkley Sound's climate is classified as "coastal temperate." Understanding west coast weather is very important to the safety and enjoyment of your trip. This section provides an overview of weather factors to take into account in your trip planning.

JET STREAM

The jet stream, a wind pattern high in the atmosphere, has a strong influence on west coast weather patterns. Low pressure systems are associated with bad weather and high pressures systems with good weather. In winter the prevailing jet stream moves south, drawing relatively stable low pressure systems from the Gulf of Alaska along with it. This makes winters on the west coast rainy and windy, with frequent storms. During the summer, the jet stream shifts north, causing the relatively stable high pressure systems from the coast of California to bring drier and sunnier weather.

In British Columbia, 1013 millibars (101.3 kilopascals) is considered average or neutral pressure. Anything below this is considered low pressure; anything above is considered high pressure.

TEMPERATURE

The average depth of the Pacific Ocean is 3,940 m (12,900 ft), and its average temperature is 3.36°C (38°F). In Barkley Sound the surface water temperature fluctuates between 8°C (46°F) in January and 14°C (57°F) in August. The air temperature is mild in winter and warm in summer, with the annual temperature range in Ucluelet being 5–18°C (41–64°F). The Kuroshio Current, also known as the Japanese Current, helps make the climate of Vancouver Island the mildest in Canada (MacFarlane *et al*, 1996:11). Despite the seemingly mild temperature in Barkley Sound, hypothermia is still a serious threat and kayakers must have the equipment and knowledge to avoid it, or treat it in the event of an emergency.

PRECIPITATION

Precipitation on the west coast is among the heaviest in the world. The BGI receives an average of 300 cm (9.8 ft) of rain per year. Snow is rare, except at higher elevations. June through September is the "dry season," averaging 47 cm (18.5 in) of precipitation during this time (16% of total annual precipitation). The wettest recorded place in North America is Henderson Lake, located 22 km northeast of Gibraltar Island, which receives on average a whopping 655 cm (21.5 ft) of precipitation per year. The most precipitation in Canadian history was recorded there: 41.5 cm (16 in) of rain on one day in December, 1926 (Obee, 1998:11). In 1996, 902.7 cm (30 ft) of precipitation was recorded at Henderson Lake. No wonder many people call the west coast the "wet" coast.

The west coast of Vancouver Island receives much more precipitation than the east side, because the central Vancouver Island mountain range and the Olympic Mountains in Washington state create a "rain shadow" effect. As warm, moist air moves inland from the ocean, it is forced upward when it reaches the mountains. The air cools as it rises and its moisture condenses, forming clouds and, consequently, rain. Ucluelet, on the island's west coast, receives over five times more rain than Victoria, situated in the rain shadow on the east side of the island.

If your clothes get wet during your expedition, it can be very difficult to dry them out in continuing wet weather. High-quality rubber raingear (two pieces, top and bottom, are preferred) is essential to ensure comfort and safety, as is at least one tarp to string up as a rain shelter in camp. Test your raingear at home in your shower. If you're still dry after five minutes, your gear is west-coast worthy. Don't forget — even if summer is the dry season, the BGI is still rainforest country, and though the climate seems mild it is alarmingly easy to become hypothermic.

Don't rely on cotton clothes on your kayak trip. Once wet, cotton dries by absorbing body heat and takes a long time to dry. You will lose nine times more body heat when wearing wet cotton than if you were bare-skinned. Clothing made of wool, fleece, polyester, or polypropylene is more suitable.

Peacock Channel in the early morning. Photo: JF Marleau

MARINE WEATHER FORECAST

Marine weather forecasts are issued four times a day for the west coast of Vancouver Island: 4:00 a.m., 10:30 a.m., 4:00 p.m. and 9:30 p.m. It is important to listen to updates on a regular basis because west coast weather can change surprisingly quickly, and unexpected changes in the forecast could affect your trip planning. Listen to the marine weather forecast on VHF radio channel 21B (161.65 MHz), or on your cell phone by calling (250) 726-3415.

Marine forecasts are given for large areas, and variations exist from site to site within a given forecast area. For example, weather conditions in the BGI are generally more sheltered than those experienced in its larger forecast area, called West Coast Vancouver Island South. The weather reports from Cape Beale lighthouse, Amphitrite Point lighthouse, and the buoy at La Pérouse Bank are given as part of the marine weather report and have particular relevance to paddlers in the BGI. La Pérouse Bank is located 25 nautical miles west of Barkley Sound, and its weather report generally indicates what weather is heading toward the BGI in the next few hours. Your expedition planning should take into consideration the current marine forecast, along with your local observations and the skills and experience of your group members.

The following table provides a general idea of what to look for when assessing weather in the BGI. The presence of three or four indicators in the appropriate column indicates if the weather is likely to deteriorate, remain stable or improve.

Weather Prediction Table

Indicator	Deteriorating	Stable	Improving
Barometric pressure	Falling	Stable	Rising
Wind speed	• Increasing • strongest winds near the centre of the low pressure system	• stable	• increasing then decreasing • strongest winds near the edge of the high pressure system
Wind direction	• backing, southeast, east, south	• stable	• veering, northwest, west
Clouds and precipitation	• building cloud cover • increase in precipitation • halo around the sun or moon	• stable	• clearing cloud cover • decrease in precipitation

Adapted from Sea Kayak Instruction & Leadership Systems (SKILS). 2005:p4

View of the BGI from Mount Ozzard, near Ucluelet. Photo: JF Marleau

Make sure you know how to use a compass if you do not have a guide.
Photo: Barbara Schramm

Navigation

The Broken Group contains over 100 islands, with myriad channels large and small between them. It is easy for kayakers to get lost if they are not prepared. This section provides general information on navigating in the BGI, including the many factors that kayakers should factor into their ongoing navigation decisions, such as tides, wind, waves, swell, fog and surf. But remember that reading about navigation is not the same as doing it. You would be well advised to learn the tools and techniques of kayak navigation from a class or book. Kayaking the BGI is an excellent way to put that learning into practice.

CHARTS

The Canadian Hydrographic Service offers two charts that cover the BGI: numbers 3670 and 3671. Chart 3670 (scale 1:20,000) includes the BGI and the northwest region of Barkley Sound. It shows more detail in the BGI than chart 3671 (scale 1:40,000). Chart 3671 is suitable if you plan to paddle to or from Ucluelet, the Deer Group or Bamfield. Otherwise, 3670 is the better chart to have. *Do not* use the maps in this book for navigation — they are for information only. When navigating with your chart, look for micro-features such small islands, channel markers, lights, buoy, bays, inlets, campsites, beaches, etc.

Your chart is fundamental to your safety. Make sure you have a good chart case to protect it. One recommended chart case looks like a giant Ziploc bag big enough to contain the chart folded in half. That way you won't have to repeatedly fold and refold a chart, which saves time and frustration. It will also keep your chart from getting wet and ripping.

You can obtain charts 3670 and 3671 from marine agents or from:

Canadian Hydrographic Service
Pacific Coast Distribution Office
9860 Saanich Road, Sidney, BC
V8L 4B2   (250) 363-6358

TIDES

"Do you hear water"?

Andrew Woodford

Tides are a fact of life in the BGI, one ignored at the kayaker's peril. The tidal range in the BGI is 4.3 m (14 feet). The tides are mixed semidiurnal, meaning there are two low tides and two high tides of different heights each day.

Tide tables, based on mathematical models, predict the height and the time of the tides. The tables are usually accurate, but do not take other natural influences into account. For example, a barometric pressure change of 30 millibars can cause water levels to rise or fall by roughly 30 cm. Low pressure systems cause water levels to rise, while high pressure systems cause the opposite.

Tide tables are available on the Internet (www.lau.chs-shc.dfo-mpo.gc.ca) or by purchasing the **Canadian Tide and Current Tables Volume 6** for Discovery Passage and the West Coast of Vancouver Island (cost under $8 CDN at time of writing). The tidal reference station for the BGI is Tofino. Secondary stations are located at Effingham Bay and Stopper Islands, but the differences between the reference and secondary stations are marginal. Remember that the tide table uses Pacific Standard Time — add an hour to the listed time during daylight savings!

Always consider the tide when setting up camp. It's far from pleasant to find your tent beginning to float on an incoming tide at three in the morning. And always tie your boat to something immovable during the night to keep the tide from spiriting it away. Hope for the best, but plan for the worst.

WIND

The prevailing wind during the summer is from the northwest, which indicates good weather. Bad weather usually comes with wind from the southeast or south. Summer winds in Barkley Sound generally pick up around 11 a.m. and die around 6 p.m. The best time to cross large channels, of course, is when it is calm.

David Channel on a calm day. Photo: JF Marleau

WAVES AND SWELL

Wind directly influences waves and swell. Large swell or wind waves can make your expedition very challenging, especially on longer crossings. Wind waves (chop) are generally close together and relatively short and steep. They do not travel very far and dissipate when the wind dies down. Swells are long, smooth, regular waves that are leftovers from distant storms. They can be deceptively high, and can travel for long periods of time over huge distances on the open ocean. Swell is uncommon in most parts of the sheltered inner islands of the Broken Group.

Paddling the west and south sides of Wouwer, Howell, Cree, Benson and Batley Islands or the south side of Effingham is for advanced paddlers only. These areas can have significant swells, strong winds and many boomers[2]. Be aware of confused seas close to these shores. Keep a safe distance off, especially when the swell is moderate to heavy.

Crossing Imperial Eagle and Loudoun Channels to the BGI is also only for advanced kayakers, because of the swell and chop. The crossing should only be attempted in the early morning when the sea state is flat and the winds are weak.

David Channel can also be challenging. Coaster Channel, which creates a natural boundary between the outer and the inner islands[3], can be another nasty surprise for paddlers. Though usually calm on summer mornings, the sea state builds in the afternoon, making the crossing more difficult. It is not uncommon for kayakers visiting the outer islands to be unable to cross Coaster Channel to regain their campsite in the inner islands. In this case it is advised to radio for a water taxi. The outer islands offer more dramatic scenery than the inner, but the price for paddlers is higher risk.

---

[2] A boomer is where large waves break periodically over a shallow rock.
[3] Owens, Clarke and Benson Islands are considered part of the outer islands.

Fog rolling in at Gilbert Island campsite. Photo: JF Marleau

FOG

Fog is very common during the summer, especially in August (locally known as "Foggust"). There are two types of fog you may encounter in the Broken Group: radiation fog and sea fog. Radiation fog forms on land in early morning when water vapour in the air cools and condenses over the cold land. It is generally blown away by wind or is burned off by the sun as the day heats up. Sea fog (also called advection fog) develops when warm, moist air moves over cold water. The water vapour condenses and creates fog. This type of fog will often form offshore and move in toward the BGI. You can often see the thick, low wall of white fog coming from a long distance. It can roll in quickly.

When navigating by compass in the fog, aim for large islands. Always double-check your bearing, and play safe by allowing a generous margin for error. Don't forget magnetic variation (the difference between true and magnetic north, printed on the chart's compass rose) and make sure there is no deviation error caused by, for instance, a steel ruler or VHF radio stowed near the compass. Stay calm and trust your compass, not your instinct. Use dead reckoning (speed, distance and time) to keep track of your progress.

In the worst case, if you become completely disoriented in the BGI, simply head north and you will eventually reach land, where you can beach on a safe shore and wait for the fog to clear. Keep the members of your group very close to each other in foggy conditions and travel near shore when possible.

The Long Beach area is a better place than the Broken Group Islands for surf kayaking within the national park. Photo: Barbara Schramm

SURF KAYAKING

The BGI and northwest Barkley Sound are generally not a good place for surf kayaking. However, during moderate or heavy swell you will encounter surf on the beaches of Benson, Clark and Dicebox Islands. The west side of Lovett Island has steep swells with consistent surf, but this site is rocky and dangerous and therefore not recommended for surf kayaking.

Fishing and shellfish harvesting

Seafood exists in abundance in the BGI, and many kayakers take advantage of this to harvest a meal or two. A salt-water fishing licence (under $30 CDN at time of printing) is required to fish or to harvest shellfish in Canadian tidal waters, including the BGI. Catch/harvest limits are set and periodically adjusted by the Department of Fisheries and Oceans (DFO) and Parks Canada. At time of printing, the catch limit in the BGI for shellfish was 12 per day, which includes all species combined (for example, six California mussels, three blue mussels and three oysters). It is illegal to harvest abalone in British Columbia, or to harvest shellfish in a closed area.

The BGI is DFO management area 23–8. Lyall Point is area 23–9, and north of Toquart Bay is area 23–10.

PARALYTIC SHELLFISH POISONING

Paralytic shellfish poisoning (PSP), also known as "red tide," only affects bivalve shellfish such as oysters, mussels, clams and scallops. It does not affect crabs, prawns or shrimp. PSP is caused by particular species of dinoflagellates (a kind of plankton) experiencing a bloom, or population explosion, usually due to a period of prolonged sunshine in the summer. (Not all dinoflagellates are harmful — some create bioluminescence, lighting up the water at night when agitated by movement.) A plankton bloom will sometimes make the water look reddish brown. Note that periods of heavy rain can flush natural dyes from cedar trees into the ocean, also making the water brown, so water colour is not a reliable indication of a bloom.

During a red tide the dinoflagellate toxins accumulate in the flesh of bivalves that feed by filtering plankton from the water, the toxins accumulate in their tissues. The toxins don't affect the bivalve but are poisonous to warm-blooded animals. Cooking does not destroy the toxins.

Eating PSP-contaminated shellfish could kill you. The first effects of eating contaminated shellfish are a tingling feeling in the lips and tongue. This is followed by numbness in toes and fingers, and then loss of muscle control. In a serious case of PSP, you have an emergency on your hands! Induce vomiting and call the park wardens immediately. Always check with DFO for any closures due to red tide or other contamination.

Chinook salmon caught at Swale Rock.

FISHING

There are 34 species of inshore rockfish in British Columbia. Depending on species, rockfish can live up to 170 years and reach sexual maturity at seven to 20 years of age. Stocks of inshore rockfish are presently at a low level, and Parks Canada has closed all finfish fishing in most of the BGI to protect rockfish and facilitate their recovery. Studies have shown that a rockfish, when caught, brought to the surface and released, will likely die. Catch-and-release is thus not an effective strategy for rockfish protection. This is why most of the Broken Group is closed to all finfish fishing.

Check with park wardens or look for notices posted on the campground privies prior to fishing in the BGI. There are a few good spots in the Broken Group still open to fishing. The west side of Benson Island is very good for coho and chinook salmon from July to September. The south and east sides of Effingham Island are good for coho during the summer, and for Chinook from spring through fall. Swale Rock is good for coho during the summer, Chinook during the summer through fall, and sockeye in June. Barkley Sound is famous for its world-class sportfishing.

Department of Fisheries and Oceans
(office in Port Alberni)
(250) 724-0195
Office hours Monday to Friday, 8 a.m. to 4 p.m.

Paralytic Shellfish Poisoning (PSP) Hotline,
for current closure information: (604) 666-2828

First Nations history and culture

The Nuu-chah-nulth are the First Nations people who inhabit the west coast of Vancouver Island, from Brooks Peninsula (in the north) to the northwest corner of Washington state (in the south). Nuu-chah-nulth means "people living along the mountains" in the Nuu-chah-nulth language. At present there are 15 different Nuu-chah-nulth nations. From north to south they are: Kyuquot/Cheklesaht, Ehattesaht, Nuchatlaht, Mowachaht/Muchalaht, Hesquiaht, Ahousaht, Tla-o-qui-aht, Ucluelet, Toquaht, Tseshaht, Uchucklesaht, Hupacasath, Ohiaht, Ditidaht and Makah.

Six of these nations claim Barkley Sound as part of their traditional territory: the Ucluelet, Toquaht, Tseshaht, Ohiaht, Uckucklesaht and Hupacasath bands.

Barkley Sound's temperate climate and abundance of food were the major factors in sustaining a Nuu-chah-nulth population larger than at other locations on the west coast of Vancouver Island. It also fostered the development of an advanced culture.

The Tseshaht were not the only aboriginal group to have lived in the BGI, but today they are the only remaining Nuu-chah-nulth group that once did. They are an amalgamation of at least six independent groups from the central region of Barkley Sound (Inglis, 1986:113). Tseshaht translates to "people who smell of rotting whales on the beach."

No written records of First Nations history exist prior to European contact. Nuu-chah-nulth history is oral, passed down from generation to generation through songs, stories, dances and rituals. The first part of this chapter describes the life and culture of the Nuu-chah-nulth people. The second part focuses on Tseshaht history.

Nuu-chah-nulth way of life

The Nuu-chah-nulth people all shared a similar way of life, but were separated into major tribes, or confederated groups of tribes, many of which warred with each other. The BGI has approximately 170 archaeological sites that have shed light on the aboriginal way of life.

The Nuu-chah-nulth people lived in a society of strongly ranked social groups, in which class and rank played a major role in one's life. For example, marriage was considered an alliance of families, arranged by parents with important consideration given to social status. Slaves, mainly women and children captured in war, were at the bottom of the social ladder. Men were usually killed because they could pose a threat to their captors. War captives were sometimes tortured. Slaves were considered property that could be bought, sold, mistreated or killed. Slaves were forced to eat shellfish to test for poisonous red tide.

The Tseshaht, as well as many other Nuu-chah-nulth groups, followed "typical Nootka mortuary practices of placing the dead in trees on small islands, or in caves and rock shelters at some distance from the village" (McMillan and St.Claire, 1982:46). It is common along the west coast of Vancouver Island to find old burial sites, with bones or small cedar burial boxes inside caves or placed underneath rocky outcrops. Unfortunately these sites were and still are plagued by vandalism and thievery. It is illegal and unethical to remove artefacts or buried human remains! If you find a burial site please respect it.

CEDAR

The western red cedar was the "tree of life" for Nuu-chah-nulth people. They used every part of the cedar for many purposes — building houses and canoes, making rope, weaving clothing, baskets, carpets and diapers, etc. The Nuu-chah-nulth were able to extract planks and bark from cedar trees without killing the tree. Some of those trees are still alive and can be seen in the BGI and greater Barkley Sound. Such a living artefact is called a culturally modified tree or CMT.

Culturally modified tree. Photo: JF Marleau

Dugout canoes were made from whole cedar trees. To do this, the Nuu-chah-nulth burned out the base of a large cedar tree, putting wet clay on the trunk above the fire to keep it from spreading. Once the tree had fallen, the inside was carved out. Dugout canoes were made during the winter and finished in the spring.

FOOD

First Nations in the BGI had a diverse supply of food, including land mammals, berries, plants, shellfish, marine mammals and fish. The sea provided most of their food. Fish such as halibut, cod, herring, dogfish, anchovy and salmon were eaten frequently.

Salmon was an important diet staple for the Nuu-chah-nulth. Salmon traps were made with rocks or wood and set on tidal flats at river mouths where salmon aggregated before going upstream to spawn. There are no salmon creeks in the BGI but there are several in greater Barkley Sound. Salmon was often smoked so it would keep it for long periods.

The Nuu-chah-nulth people used fish traps as an efficient way to catch large numbers of small fish such as herring, anchovy, pilchard and perch.

The fish traps consisted of rock walls with a small entranceway. The Nuu-chah-nulth chased fish into the enclosure with their canoes by slapping the water with sticks to scare the fish toward the trap. Once the fish were inside, the entrance was obstructed with a cedar plank or a wooden weir. The water could escape but the fish could not. The Nuu-chah-nulth waited for the tide to drop and gathered up the stranded fish.

Fish trap on Jaques Island.
Photo: JF Marleau

The remains of 39 fish traps of indeterminate age have been found in the BGI, though only seven are still easily visible. All are located in sheltered

Figure 7 — Fish traps

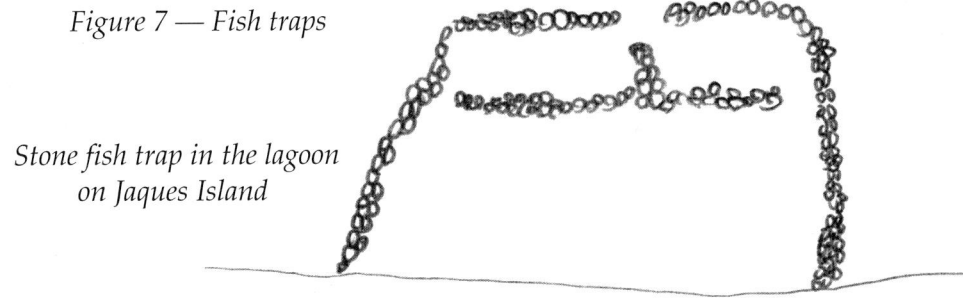

Stone fish trap in the lagoon on Jaques Island

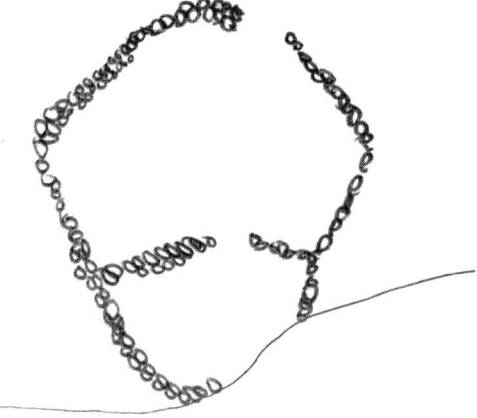

Stone fish trap on Brabant Island and in the lagoon on Jaques Island

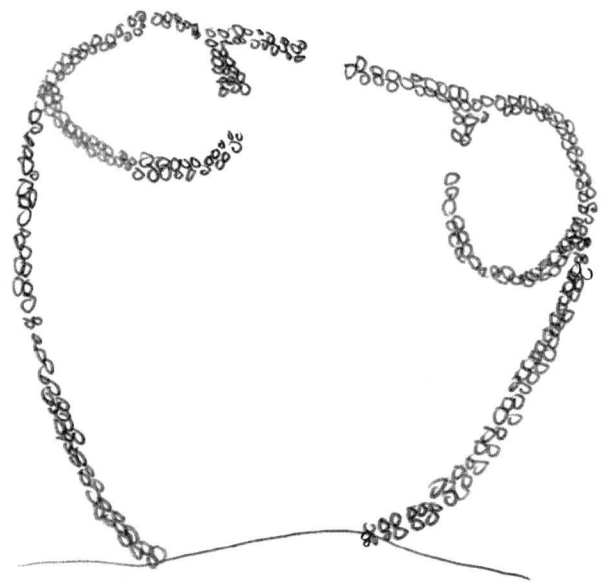

Stone fish trap on Mence Island

bays: three in the lagoon between Jacque and Jarvis Islands, and four others on Brabant, Mence, Turtle and Wouwer Islands.

Shellfish was a secondary source of food, one especially important during the winter when bad weather limited fishing and hunting. Shellfish could be gathered year round except during red tides, which usually occurred during the summer.

WHALING

First Nations ate whales, both those they killed themselves and recently dead whales that drifted ashore. Whales and whaling were an important part of First Nations culture, as an inspiration for art and a source of pride and glory for the people. The First Nations in Barkley Sound primarily hunted humpback whales, which were larger, more plentiful, and had more oil than other species. Killer whales were too difficult to hunt and were only targeted by young whalers in training.

A whale hunting crew was composed of eight to ten people in the canoe: the chief (always the harpooner), a person to steer, and six to eight paddlers. Floats made of sealskin were attached to the harpoon by a long rope, making it difficult for the harpooned whale to dive and harder for it to swim. Once it tired, the chief then gave the fatal strike with a short spear. At once a crew member dove into the water, cut a hole through the whale's upper lip and jaw, and tied the mouth shut to keep the carcass from filling with water.

The crew then began the exhausting work of towing the 40-ton animal back to shore. If a hunt was not successful it was believed to be a result of not properly observing rituals.

Whaling Canoe on display at the Wickaninnish Interpretive Centre, PRNPR. Photo: B. Schramm

MIDDENS

There are 32 recorded midden sites in the Broken Group and along Sechart Channel (McMillan and St.Claire, 1982:29). Middens are essentially First Nations' garbage dumps, where unusable items and the inedible parts of food animals (such as shells) were discarded. Middens are often located near beaches and other habitation sites. They look like mounds of dark soil with a lack of vegetative cover and many pieces of shell inside. Their size depends on the length and intensity of occupation of the site. Middens are considered archaeological sites and are protected by provincial and federal laws. Archaeologists excavate middens to better understand the culture and history of First Nations. It is unlawful to dig into a midden without permission.

EUROPEAN CONTACT

The first European to exchange goods with the Nuu-chah-nulth was Captain James Cook, who arrived at Friendly Cove, Nootka Sound, in 1778. Cook stayed for one month. Four years prior to this, first contact had been made by Spanish captain Juan Perez and his crew, who stopped only for one night and did not go ashore for fear of being attacked. In the years following Cook other explorers came to trade in Barkley Sound.

Unfortunately, contact with the Europeans brought devastating diseases such as influenza, typhoid, measles, whooping cough, venereal disease and, the worst of all, smallpox. First Nations people had no natural immunity against these new diseases. Two-thirds of the Nuu-chah-nulth population died, primarily due to smallpox. The arrival of Europeans and their diseases cataclysmically affected Nuu-chah-nulth life, triggering a domino effect of wars, tribal amalgamations, and the relocation of many villages.

First Nations on Effingham Island around 1930. Copyright PRNPR Archives

Tseshaht History

Archaeological digs on Benson Island between 1999 and 2001 show signs of occupation by First Nations people for more than 5,000 years. Though there is no scientific evidence that the Tseshaht were the first group to inhabit the island, in their creation story the Tseshaht consider Benson Island to be the birthplace of their people. The main Tseshaht villages were on Benson Island, with the higher ranking members of the tribe living in a village on the north side of the island and the lower ranking in a village on the east side.

For thousands of years the traditional Tseshaht territory included Benson, Clark, Owens, Lovett, Trickett and Turret Islands, plus a portion of Batley Island, as well as all the waters surrounding them. For most of their existence prior to the last 200 years, the Tseshaht were confined to this small cluster of islands until they expanded it through warfare.

Warfare played a large role in traditional Nuu-chah-nulth culture. A major cause of war was for control of territory with important natural resources, such as salmon streams. Ownership of land changed depending on the outcomes of the wars. According to Nuu-chah-nulth tradition, once a group surrendered its autonomy their entire territory was given to the dominant group. War, alliance and amalgamation had important social and political consequences (McMillan and St.Claire, 2003:40).

Though these territorial shifts occurred prior to the coming of the Europeans, they likely accelerated after contact. "The introduction of a new set of economic priorities and relationships with the inception of the maritime fur trade produced considerable intergroup tensions as various groups strove to profit from and, wherever possible, dominate trade relations with Europeans" (St.Claire, NA:23).

The Tseshaht fared well in these conflicts. "With the completion of a series of amalgamations early in the nineteenth century, the Tseshaht world was fundamentally transformed.... In only a few decades ... they had absorbed numerous neighbouring groups" (McMillan and St.Claire, 2003:40). At its pinnacle at the end of the nineteenth century the Tseshaht had become the dominant group in Barkley Sound, significantly increasing the size of their traditional territory to include most of Barkley Sound — all the Broken Group Islands, the west side of the Deer Group, most of the north shore of the sound, most of the Alberni Canal, and the lower part of the Somass River. With this larger territory, they were able to exploit more natural resources.

These amalgamations resulted in a decline in the number of independent groups and an increase in territory size for surviving groups. A seasonal pattern of moving between winter and summer villages was developed to utilize the larger territories (Inglis and Haggarty, 1986:218). By the beginning of the 1800s, only a summer village was located on Benson Island (Arima et al, 1991:141). For much of that century the main Tseshaht village was located on Effingham Island, where the lake was important for ceremonial activities (Arima et al, 1991:149).

The main villages were mostly located in sheltered areas, but people regularly moved to outlying camps where they could harvest fish, shellfish and other resources. Tseshaht lived in longhouses made of cedar. Their main winter village was located by the Somass River at the head of Alberni Inlet (where Port Alberni is situated today). This place offered an excellent salmon river and a location more sheltered from winter storms than the BGI.

From March to August the Tseshaht lived in the Broken Group. In August they started a slow migration toward the Somass River for the winter; in January they began moving in the opposite direction, their movements following the availability of food sources (McMillan and St.Claire, 1982:22). Though their longhouse foundations were permanently set in the ground, the roof and walls were made of large, detachable cedar planks. The group literally moved house, removing the planks and transporting them by canoe to the permanent foundations that stood at the other seasonal villages.

First Nations' village on Keith Island around 1915. Copyright PRNPR Archives

The Tseshaht abandoned their villages in the Broken Group in the early 1800s and returned in the 1840s (Inglis and Haggarty, 1986:277-279). When the federal government gave land to the Nuu-chah-nulth in 1882, the Tseshaht were actively using three areas in the BGI (on Effingham, Nettle and Keith Islands). These islands were given to the Tseshaht as Indian reserves. Benson Island was not given reservation status because there were no visible signs of Tseshaht occupation. When John Benson bought the island in 1903 the Tseshaht occasionally visited Benson Island.

The Tseshaht and other Nuu-chah-nulth groups were not able to freely inhabit Barkley Sound after the creation of the reserves; they only had control of their reserve land, and with increasing government control their lives changed dramatically. The Tseshaht, who used to be conquerors in Barkley Sound, were conquered by the federal government without war or physical aggression (Ingles and Haggarty, 1986:97).

In 1914, the major Tseshaht village on Effingham Island burned, the fire apparently started by someone attempting to burn snakes out of their dens and losing control of the blaze. Later, in the 1940s, the Tseshaht reserve by the Somass River in Port Alberni became (and remains to this day) their main settlement. Tseshaht do not live in the BGI today, though they commercially harvest shellfish on Equis beach and often use the cabins and dock on Nettle Island. Otherwise, the BGI is not a significant place for Tseshaht to live, work or recreate.

The long history of disease and warfare caused a dramatic decline in the Tseshaht population, which plunged steadily from the 1780s to the 1930s, until finally beginning to recover in the late 1980s (Arima et al, 1991:1). Now the Tseshaht have a much higher birth rate than the rest of British Columbia's population.

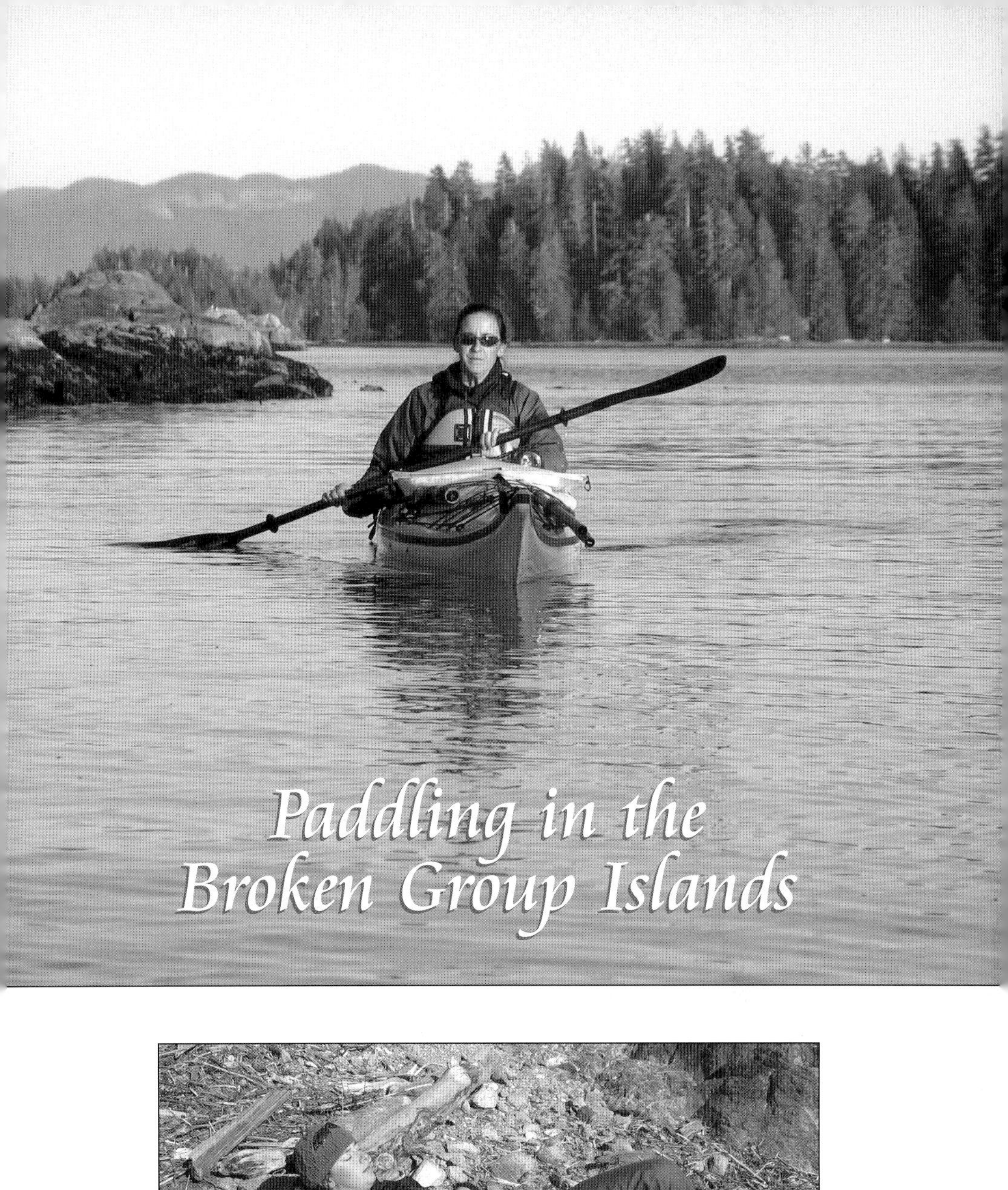

Paddling in the Broken Group Islands

A nap after lunch is a good way to enjoy your trip. Photos: JF Marleau

Hand Island is often the first stop in the BGI for kayakers launching from Toquart Bay. Photo: JF Marleau

HAND, BRABANT AND MENCE ISLANDS

Paddling along the shore of these three islands is relatively sheltered, except for their west sides. The campsite on the east side of Hand Island is usually the first stop for kayakers entering the BGI because it is the closest campsite to Toquart Bay. Toquart Bay campground is five nautical miles (9.25 km) from Hand Island when paddling the shortest possible distance. During ideal sea states and weather conditions, it will take between an hour and a half to three hours depending on the skills and fitness levels of the group. An average group paddles two knots per hour (3.7 km). The campsite on Hand has two nice sandy beaches. The main beach, the larger of the two, is accessible from the north and south at any tide. The second and smaller beach is on the east side of the island; at low tide, kayaks must be carried ashore over the boulders.

The channel between the east side of Hand Island and Island 34 (the one with a flashing white light) can be traversed at medium or high tide. Another sandy beach is located on the northwest side of Hand, just south of some boomers. This is a suitable rest or lunch spot.

Captain Richard named the island after Henry Hand, an officer working on a survey vessel under Captain Richard's command. There was a house and trading post on Hand Island around 1900. The McKay family managed the trading posts on Hand and Gilbert Islands and traded with the First Nations from Sechart, Dodger Cove and Nettle, Turret, and Effingham Islands.

Former McKay's house on Hand Island. Copyright PRNPR Archives

Most of Hand was logged by settlers, so the forested area there now is mostly second growth. The McKays hauled the fallen timber into the water

McKay's donkey engine. Photo: JF Marleau

with donkey engines. If you hike the trail to the Hand Island lagoon you can see abandoned logging equipment and an old, rusty donkey engine.

The Brabant Islands have a small arch on their west side which can be seen at low tide. The small bay on the east side contains the remains of a fish trap. The Brabants also have a sandy beach on their southeast side at low tide. The Geographic Board of Canada changed the name of the island from Pender to Brabant in 1905, honouring Father Brabant, a Roman Catholic missionary from Belgium who worked on the west coast in 1875.

Paddlers can explore the channel between the Brabant Islands and the channel between Brabant and Mence Islands at low tide. There is a fish trap on the north side of Mence Island.

CHALK, DODD, WILLIS, AND TURTLE ISLANDS AND THE TINY GROUP

This cluster of islands (with the exception of the Tiny Group) is a popular, sheltered anchorage for motorboats during the summer. One entrance to this harbour is a small channel between Dodd and Chalk Islands. It conceals a rock pinnacle that is occasionally rammed at high tide by motorboats.

Chalk Island (formerly Price Island) has a sandy beach on its northern point, which shows up well enough to be used as a bearing when crossing Peacock Channel from the Brabant Islands. The beach is suitable for landing at low or medium tide. There is a clearing with a small midden behind Island 7 on the west side of Chalk. The beach is very rocky.

The Dodd and Willis Islands campsites are very popular, particularly for commercial groups, due to their central location. They are the most crowded campsites in the BGI. The beach by Dodd's campsite is located on the eastern tip of the island, facing Walsh Island. The campsite is located on a narrow peninsula and offers views of a sheltered harbour on one side and Peacock Channel on the other. Dodd used to be a First Nations' village site. It has a large midden which spreads from the campsite toward the southwest along the shore. The trail behind the privies goes to a meadow where there is a small creek.

There are two sandy beaches located on Dodd Island, one on the northwest side of the island and the other facing the campsite on Willis Island. The latter is called Moonsnail Beach because of the numerous moonsnails found there. The narrow channel between Dodd and Willis is a great place for tidepooling. Boisterous "gap winds" frequently funnel through this narrow channel in the afternoon with the rising northwesterly winds.

Willis Island campsite.
Photo: JF Marleau

The campsite on Willis has two separate beaches. The best spot to camp is at the point between the two beaches, which offers more privacy and great views of the sunset. Access to the Willis Island privies at high tide is difficult, though, and you may get wet feet. A giant western red cedar grew here for centuries, leaning at a sharp angle. The tree fell one morning during the summer of 2003, narrowly missing a tent. A small midden was discovered at the base of the tree when it fell.

Willis Island has some impressive trees near the campsite. The east side of the island is second growth. Look for a carving on a cedar deadfall on Island 21 when paddling the channel between the southern tip of Willis and Island 21. It is not known who carved it, or when. Paddling along this

Before it collapsed in 2003, this giant western red cedar on Willis Island grew for centuries at a 45-degree angle. Photo: JF Marleau

shoreline is good for tidepooling at low tide.

The Tiny Group is a must-see. A seal colony inhabits the rocks to the northwest of the islets. Two beaches are nestled in the Tiny Group. On the northern island (24), the beach faces north and therefore doesn't receive much sunlight. The other beach (on Island 8) is more exposed. The latter is made

The Tiny Group. JF Marleau

of eroded shells, making it one of the most beautiful beaches in the BGI.

The remains of a fish trap are located on the northwest side of Turtle, by Island 7, though you have to look hard to recognize them. Two gravel beaches, one on the northeast and the other on the east side of Turtle, can be used as rest stops. Joe's Bay also has several places to land.

Salal Joe's floating cabin and docks. Copyright PRNPR Archives

Turtle Island was home to the legendary Salal Joe for 21 years. Salal Joe harvested salal and ferns (used by commercial florists in their arrangements), which he loaded onto the M.V. *Lady Rose* for shipment to Vancouver Island and Lower Mainland florists. He also harvested clams and sold them to Bamfield processors.

Salal Joe's real name was Joe Wilkowski. Though written articles claimed he was from Poland, Iraq or Iran, Joe's friends maintain he was born in Russia. Salal Joe did not talk much about his past, even with close friends. He came to Canada as an illegal immigrant during or after World War II but never applied for Canadian citizenship. He worked different jobs, keeping a low profile.

Salal Joe's garden on Dodd Island. Copyright PRNPR Archives

Salal Joe's boat Hello Nature. *Copyright PRNPR Archives*

In 1959 he built a floating cabin and dock in a small bay now called Joe's Bay. The cabin was impeccably clean and he lived there as a hermit with his cat, Chico. He rarely went to town, and never visited a hospital or clinic. Fortunately he had a dentist friend who stopped in the Broken Group every year to check his teeth.

Joe liked fishing to feed himself and Chico. He also grew fruits and vegetables in a garden on Dodd Island, which he fenced with wood and netting to keep out the deer. The remains of his garden are located to the left of the trail leading to the privies. Some poles and fruit trees are still standing, and the fence and a fishnet lay near the bush line. The native

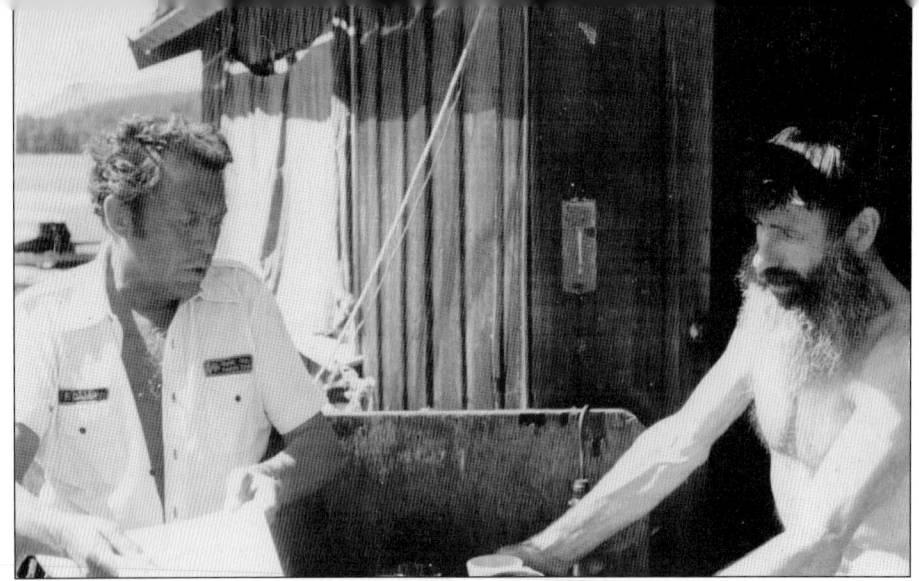

Salal Joe with Frank Camp, former Park superintendent.
Copyright PRNPR Archives

vegetation is slowly growing back, and now the trees create shade where the garden once was.

When the Broken Group unit of the national park was established in 1973, everyone living in the islands was evicted except for Salal Joe. An informal agreement stipulated that he could stay in the islands as long his presence did not become an issue, and he was contracted by Parks Canada to demolish cabins on the islands and to build campsite facilities.

Salal Joe hid from strangers and avoided police and government personnel, with the exception of park wardens such as Gord McClean, the first warden, who patrolled the islands for 15 years, and Frank Camp, then park superintendent, both of whom were his good friends. Joe was the unofficial guardian of the BGI, aware of all comings and goings in Barkley Sound, and worked collaboratively with the wardens.

One day Joe had an unusual experience which interfered with his caretaker duties. When he arrived on Clark Island he saw six naked women. Being shy even around clothed strangers, he was at a loss as to what to do. Joe tracked down Brian Congdon, then a park warden, and got him to tell the women to dress themselves so he could get his work done.

Though Joe had many friends, mostly fishermen, he was deeply suspicious of strangers. Visitors frequently stopped at his cabin but he often locked his door and ignored them. He hated when people tried to take his photograph. Only those he knew well were welcome. Despite his peculiarities, those who knew him described him as being friendly, polite, and a gentleman. They often stopped by to bring him sugar, coffee and alcohol.

The legendary Salal Joe.
Copyright PRNPR Archives

Joe died mysteriously in 1980, at the age of about 65 (no one knew his real age). Apparently he was partying on the night of his accident — he could not live without his rum, gin and wine — and he never made it back to his cabin. No one knows for sure what happened, but Joe's boat, an old wooden scow named *Hello Nature*, was found on the north side of Chalk Island with the throttle wide open. Joe never wore a PFD or carried safety equipment on board. After his death, Joe's cabin was towed to Bamfield. A few rusty pieces of equipment and a fresh-water well remain in Joe's Bay.

GIBRALTAR, JAQUES, JARVIS AND TREBLE ISLANDS

Gibraltar is a popular place for kayakers travelling on the M.V. *Frances Barkley* because it's the closest campsite to Sechart. There are several decent spots to set up tents, the best located on the little forested hill on the north side of the beach. Commercial group don't often use Gibraltar, but during peak season it is very busy at lunch time because it's one of the best places to land and is sunny. There used to be a short trail from the campsite along the north shore but now most of it is overgrown. Another short trail goes along the west side of the campsite. The campsite itself is located on a midden. During the winter and spring, or after substantial precipitation, a small waterfall forms near the southern side of the beach's campsite.

There is a pleasant lagoon on Gibraltar's west side, where at low tide you can land on a small sand beach and go swimming. In June, 2003, the remains of a small whale were found in the lagoon, with wolves feeding on the carcass. A creek flows into the lagoon from a lake, slightly smaller than the one on Effingham. The lake can be reached by following the creek. (Watch for sharp rocks and oysters in the creek bed.) The creek is quite small during the summer but fills up to one metre deep during the wet season. An

Along the shore of Jaques Island. Photo: JF Marleau

Sea cave on Gibraltar Island. Photo: JF Marleau

The lagoon between Jaques and Jarvis Islands offers sheltered water. JF Marleau

impressive number of logs float on the lake, indicative of past logging activity. The north and west sides of Gibraltar are sheltered but the east and south sides, which face Imperial Eagle Channel, are exposed. A large sea cave yawns on the south shore of the island. Look for a hidden sea arch near the cave on Gibraltar Island. Gibraltar's name was given by Captain Richards in 1861 due to its resemblance to the rock of Gibraltar in the Mediterranean Sea.

The former warden cabin was on the southeast side of Jaques Island, formerly Puzzle Island. This cabin was later used by paddlers as an emergency shelter. Only the outhouse remains. The beach is suitable for landing at low tide but there are a lot of boulders. You can find a lot of culturally modified trees in the clearing here.

The lagoon between Jaques and Jarvis is one of the most tranquil places in the BGI, its sheltered water giving the impression of paddling on a lake. Many ducks congregate on the lagoon during the winter. Four channels enter the lagoon. The southwest entrance is very narrow and requires at least seven feet of water above chart datum for a single kayak to pass through. Near this main southwest entrance, another entrance on the north side is extremely well hidden. This channel is probably the least known passage in the BGI and requires a minimum tide of 3.5 m (10.5 ft) above chart datum for a single kayak to pass through. The best way to find it is to paddle from the Tiny Group Islands towards the small lagoon on the

Paddling along the shore offers opportunities to discover intertidal life.

Lake on Gibraltar Island.
Photos: JF Marleau

southeast tip of Jarvis Island. At the back of the small lagoon, go through a narrow channel for 25 m (82.5 ft). At the end of this channel, you will reach the big lagoon between Jaques and Jarvis.

The northeast entrance always has enough water to paddle through. The choice access however, is via a small channel on the northwest of Jarvis. For an unloaded double to easily pass through the northwest passage of the lagoon, kayakers need a tide of at least 1.5 m (5 ft) above chart datum. This channel, great for tidepooling and known locally as the "aquarium," is dry at very low tide.

The lagoon was used as a food processing area by First Nations. Look for the "M" on your chart (chart 3670) — this is the muddy bay where three fish traps are located, including the two best preserved fish traps in the park. You can see them from your kayak at low tide. You can also see canoe runs, used for launching and beaching cedar canoes, in the lagoon on Jarvis Island.

Paddling along the north shores of Jaques and Jarvis is sheltered, even in strong wind. There's good tidepooling here at low tide. There's also a sheltered lagoon and an eagle's nest on the west side of Jarvis.

Often people paddle by the Treble Islands without taking the time to visit it. There's a quaint, secluded sandy beach here at low tide — a good spot for swimming.

Photo: JF Marleau

PRIDEAUX, NETTLE, DENNE AND REEKS ISLANDS

There was a copper mine and homestead on the east side of Prideaux Island, with the mineshaft being built and expanded from 1912 to 1956. The site is located near the shoreline on the southeast side of the little bay, but is not visible from the water. There is a wooden barricade around the mineshaft, and part of a foundation and retaining wall are still visible. The Crown purchased the island in 1974.

The mine was a failure because it kept flooding. The mineshaft is unfortunately now filled with garbage, and garbage dumping here has become a concern. Park wardens made an effort in 1991 to remove some of the garbage, but much still remains (Earth Tech, 2002:8). Copper was not the only resource extracted: The east of Prideaux was logged a long time ago.

The channels between Denne, Nettle and Prideaux Islands are quiet. Three sandy beaches line Nettle's north side, with another adjacent to the Indian Reserve. A dock, two cabins and a large midden are located on the reserve. These should not be used without permission. A sizeable bog sits in the middle of Nettle Island. Some logging took place on Nettle, and First Nations have cleared trees on their reserve land. Several culturally modified trees were spared and can be found on the island's north side.

Paddlers can spot a sea arch and a sea cave on the south side of Reeks Island. The northwest side of Reeks is a good place to stop for a break, but paddling the east side is exposed. The channel between Reeks and Nettle is nice to explore.

Island 30 lies between Prideaux and Nettle Islands. With a tide of 3.24 m (10.7ft) above chart datum, it's possible to paddle through a natural tunnel (approximately 7 m long) through Island 30.

MULLINS, KEITH, ONION, DEMPSTER ISLANDS AND ELBOW ISLETS

The waters between Keith, Mullins and the north side of Onion are relatively sheltered. Keith is an Indian Reserve. A midden and the remains of two canoe runs can be found on this island. Seals like to rest at low tide on the rocks on the east side of Keith and on Elbow Islet. Remember not to approach wildlife closer than 100 m. The only beach where landing is easy and permitted with a kayak in this cluster of islands is the lagoon on the east side of Dempster (formerly known as Protection Island). The sandy beach is usable at tides less than eight feet above chart datum. This beach is secluded and is ideal for swimming. A short trail leads to a beach on the other side of the island. Dempster has six sea caves with nesting cormorants. Do not enter them! The sea caves are sculpted by powerful storm waves that bite away at the softer sediment. The south shores of Dempster and Elbow are very exposed.

LOVETT, TRICKETT AND TURRET ISLANDS

The south side of this cluster of islands is moderately exposed. The north face is more protected but head winds could slow your paddling progress. The channel between Lovett and Island 30 can be crossed at any tide. These islands offer opportunities to explore and hike several sandy beaches. The loveliest, fittingly called Paradise Beach, is between Trickett and Island 30; the best time to visit is at low tide. The longer beach on the northwest tip of Turret has some clearings — a great place to stop for lunch. This beach is also a good source of driftwood for your campfire. Two other locations on Turret are also good for firewood: One is the most southerly beach, facing Coaster Channel. The second, nicknamed Wood Beach, is on the southeast side of Turret in the vicinity of an eagle's nest. Although narrow, the channel between Turret and Trickett is wide enough for a double kayak and one can paddle through on a tide of at least 9 feet. The entrance to this channel is not obvious unless you are close to shore.

The campsite on Turret is small but attractive. It sits on a large midden facing Coaster Channel and offers fabulous sunset views. The best spot to camp is on the west side of the campsite with your tent in the bush and the kitchen or common area on the beach. The forested area behind the campsite has impressive trees and is worthwhile to explore. The largest tree in the

The Giant Tree on Turret Island.
Photo: JF Marleau

BGI is a 15-minute paddle from the Turret Island campsite. To find this magnificent tree, known as the Giant Tree, from the campsite, paddle east along the shore, across the bay on your left, head toward Island 11 and look for the gravel beach on Turret Island. On the chart this beach is the notch facing the east side of Island 11. A five-minute walk along a trail leads to the tree. Be careful of the stinging nettle at the base of the hill (a midden) below the trail. Some logging, mostly along the trail to the Giant Tree, occurred in the past.

Thiepval Channel lies to the north of these islands. The channel is named after the HMCS *Thiepval*, which met its demise here. The *Thiepval* was launched in Montreal in 1917. She was named after a First World War battle in which Canadian soldiers were involved. The 39-metre vessel with its crew of 18 was used as a minesweeper by the Royal Canadian Navy until 1920. It was then stationed on the west coast and used by the Royal Canadian Navy for search and rescue, law enforcement, fishery patrols and customs regulation on the west coast of Vancouver Island.

During the 1920s and 30s, prohibition in the United States created a lucrative market for "rumrunners" — smugglers of liquor. Many vessels were involved in shipping alcohol illegally from Canada into the United States.

On the night of February 27, 1930, the HMCS *Thiepval* was on routine patrol in the BGI. After passing Lovett Island, crew members observed a suspicious boat, possibly a rumrunner, off Willis Island. As the HMCS *Thiepval* veered in pursuit, the suspect vessel tried to escape between Turtle and Turret islands. The *Thiepval* fired a warning shot from its deck gun (which is currently displayed in Ucluelet at the foot of Whiskey Dock). The *Thiepval* struck an uncharted rock during the pursuit and was stranded on a falling tide. Crew members and a second patrol vessel strove mightily to save the vessel, but unfortunately she sank the next day. The wreck now rests in 6 to 12 m of water in the channel that now bears its name. Before the BGI became part of Pacific Rim National Park Reserve the wreck was frequently looted. Now protected, it is still explored by SCUBA divers. Look for the steel loop on the rock near the wreck to tie your boat.

VILLAGE AND WIEBE ISLANDS AND FABER ISLETS

Faber Islets and Village Reef are sensitive areas. There's a seal colony here and the area is important nesting and resting habitat for birds. **Stay 100 m away from this area, and do not land here.** Use the sandy beaches on the Faber Islets only in an emergency.

Wiebe Island, formerly Randall Island, has a small gravel beach on its east side with a lagoon that is excellent for tidepooling. The best time to land on Wiebe is at low tide. Kayakers rarely go on Wiebe but it is a choice spot to have a lunch or seek some solitude. A big sea arch and a sea cave are located on the southwest side of the island. Remember, sea caves are important nesting habitat for seabirds. Because of this it is unlawful to enter sea caves in the BGI unit of Pacific Rim National Park Reserve.

BENSON AND CLARKE ISLANDS

Benson and Clarke are among the most magical islands in the BGI, and are the best for camping. However, camping here can be a challenge during rough weather, when surf landing is commonly required. In foggy conditions, be acutely aware that motorboats frequently use the channel between Benson and Clarke — sometimes at high speed.

Photo: JF Marleau

View from Benson Island. Photo: JF Marleau

Archaeological digs were conducted on Benson (formerly Hawkins Island) and Clarke (formerly Quoin Island) between 1999 and 2001. Benson was closed to campers at this time, during which three different sites were excavated. The biggest was on Benson, on a midden that proved to be over 3 m deep, indicating very long use. Clarke Island was used extensively by First Nations as a summer village. It holds five archaeological sites and several small middens (McMillan and St.Claire, 2003:22). Clarke and Benson Islands hold a significant place in Tseshaht mythology.

John Webb Benson, for whom the island is now named, was a seal hunter. In 1893 he built a two-storey, eight-bedroom hotel on the east side of the island, with a stunning view of Barkley Sound. It was busy during the summer months with visitors who came to fish and enjoy a peaceful holiday. During the winter, Benson sometimes invited friends hunting. They would arrive with dogs that drove the deer into the water, where it was easy to shoot them (Wallbank, 1991:3). Benson purchased the island in 1903 for $33. First Nations occasionally used the island during the time Benson lived there.

Benson often used his oxen to tow his boat to the nearby islands. To feed them, he cleared several acres of land for pasture. He also planted fruit trees and a garden for himself and his guests (Wallbank, 1991:2), as well as ornamental trees including chestnut, sycamore, poplar and beech (White,

Benson's hotel on Benson Island. Copyright PRNPR Archives

1974:77). Some apple and cherry trees still stand, but native vegetation grows in quickly on the west coast due to the mild climate and today only a fraction of the orchard and garden plot can be seen. Watch for the stinging nettle near the cherry and apple trees!

Benson hired a marriage broker to find him a wife to help run the hotel. The first woman to arrive left on the next boat out, for reasons unknown (Petterson, 1999:155). Benson applied again to the marriage broker — and again and again. As each woman left the island, Benson, increasingly desperate, appealed to the broker for another prospect. He struck gold with number eight and married Ella Matilda Benson, with whom he stayed until his death in 1913. Ella bought the island from Benson before he died (Wallbank, 1991:4–5). It had several more owners before it became part of Pacific Rim National Park Reserve in 1975.

Benson's hotel closed in 1922. It had at various times in its colourful history been a rendezvous for smugglers, a brothel, and a nudist colony (Wallbank,

Former cabin (now dismantled) on Clarke Island. Copyright Parks Canada

1991:12).Today, the structure is gone but the clearing where it once stood remains.

The land on Benson Island was extensively cleared by John Benson, and by First Nations prior to his arrival. A few unmarked hiking trails start from Benson's former garden. Two trails lead to a south-facing beach where you'll find a spectacular blowhole. The best "blows" occur on a rising tide during moderate to heavy swell. Be cautious when hiking along the water's edge because the rocks can be slippery. Falling into the water here could have fatal consequences.

Benson Island is the BGI's largest and least crowded campsite — the best spot to have a true wilderness experience. The campsite has two beaches: a shell-and-sand beach on the east side and a sand-with-gravel beach to the north. The best campsites are located on the south corner of the east beach. The location is private and offers views of whales and sunrises. The north site has great sunset views but can be windy. There are good whale watching opportunities from the east side of the island, as well as at nearby Sail Rock, Verbeke Reef and Pigot Islets. There's a small sea cave near the channel marker.

There used to be several cabins in the BGI but they were removed by Parks Canada for liability reasons. The last cabin to be removed was on Clarke

The monkey captured by Park Wardens on Clarke Island in 1980.
The monkey survived by stealing campers' food. Copyright Parks Canada

Island. Only the fireplace remains, along with remnants of a concrete reservoir that once collected fresh water.

William R. Clarke, the former owner of the island, imported goats with the intention that they would graze on salal. Unfortunately for him, the goats devoured everything except the salal. One day the animals actually swam off the island and were never seen again (Peterson, 1999:331). Goats were not the most exotic or unusual animal to have lived in the BGI. In 1980 park wardens captured a monkey on Clarke because it was stealing food from campers. Apparently some bright light decided to get rid of his monkey by stranding it on the island.

The Clarke Island campsite boasts the sandiest beach of all campsites in the BGI, which makes it very popular during July and August. Clarke has four beaches and a network of trails. The beaches are superb stages from which to enjoy both sunrises and sunsets. Kayakers need a tide of at least 1.35 m (4.5ft) above chart datum to cross the lagoon on the west side of Clark Island.

The beauty of Clarke Island's campsite. Photo: JF Marleau

WOUWER, BATLEY, HOWELL AND COOPER ISLANDS

Wouwer Island might have been named after Alidor Vanden Wouwer, who homesteaded on Turret Island in 1907. Wouwer Island was an important First Nations summer village site, as a base for whaling and hunting sea lions (McMillan and St.Claire, 2003:21). Fish traps are located on the southeast side of Wouwer by the "Great Tidepool" — an amazing locale for tidepool exploration and even snorkelling. A trail, not obvious, connects the north and south shores of Wouwer Island. Wouwer (formerly Storm Island) and Cooper (formerly Parker Island) have several beaches suitable for landing. Landing on Batley and Howell is more difficult. There are two sea caves on Batley's north shore and a small one on the southwest shore of Cooper. Paddling along the outer shores of Wouwer, Batley and Howell is a mosaic of rugged coastline and crashing waves.

The best wildlife spectacle in the BGI is the sea lions. These loud, smelly, quarrelsome yet highly entertaining marine mammals haul out on Wouwer, Batley and Howell Islands. There are two species of sea lions in the BGI: California and Steller. Male California sea lions are a dark chocolate brown colour, weigh up 365 kg, and are notorious for their incessant barking. Steller sea lions are larger, with males weighing up to 1,000 kg. They are lighter brown in colour and have a deep growl. Most of the sea lions in the BGI are California males (the females and pups don't migrate north). The best time to watch them is in September and October.

Wouwer Island. Photo: B. Schramm

Sea Cave on Dicebox Island.
Photo: Alan Sobey

Steller sea lions start building in numbers in July, and California sea lions begin to arrive from their breeding grounds in early August, their number increasing as the season progresses. A count in October, 2004, showed over 2,400 sea lions in the BGI! By the end of summer the sea lions are so loud they can be heard from as far away as Hand Island.

Though not very agile on land, sea lions' large front flippers propel them through the water like graceful, heavyweight torpedoes. All paddlers should maintain a distance of 100 m from sea lions, both in and out of the water. They are huge carnivores that deserve your respect.

Strangely, sea lions are more easily disturbed by kayaks than by large motor vessels. When surprised, tens and possibly hundreds of sea lions might stampede into the water in a panic — a spectacle you *don't* want to observe first-hand from a kayak. For your safety and for the wellbeing of the animals, paddling between Wouwer and Batley Islands when their shores are piled high with sea lions is *not* recommended. This is especially the case in September and October, or at high tide when more animals are in the water, having lost their haulout spots to the tide.

Slap the deck of your kayak to warn sea lions of your presence if they swim too close to your kayak. Deter them from approaching you by waving at them with your hands or paddle. If this doesn't work, slap the water aggressively with your paddle. Make sure your group stays close together. Don't stop on Wouwer's sandy beaches when sea lions are around. The animals are resting and by law are protected from being disturbed. If you observe sea lions suddenly rearing up, looking nervously toward you, and increasing their movements and vocalizations, back off slowly.

DICEBOX AND CREE ISLANDS

Dicebox is a former First Nations' defensive village used as a retreat during wars. The highest section is a promontory 35 m above the beach, which made an excellent lookout to watch for threats: A successful battle against the Ahousaht was fought here by rolling logs down the steep slopes at the attackers (McMillan and St.Claire, 2003:21). First Nations cleared land on Dicebox for their village. Inglis and Haggarty (1986:269) found evidence of 21 house platforms at this site, though dense vegetation has since grown over these platforms. Dicebox used to be a place for shellfish gathering and the hunting of cormorants (McMillan and St.Claire, 2003:21). There is a large midden on the island.

Two beaches permit kayakers to land on Dicebox. The best landing spot is the beach facing Gilbert Island, which is suitable at any tide. The beach facing Howell can only be used at high tide. Expect a surf landing on Dicebox when sea states are moderate to heavy.

Dicebox has two short trails. One heads to the bluff and the other links the island's two beaches. It also has an impressive sea cave with two mouths, a small one facing west and a larger one facing north. The latter is difficult to see from a kayak; the easiest way to view it is to hike along the island's eastern shore at low tide. Another, smaller sea cave is located on the northeast side of the island. Remember it is illegal to enter sea caves in the BGI.

Circumnavigating Cree Island (formerly Redonda Island) offers spectacular views but this route is not for the faint of heart — it's very exposed and can be dangerous, and there is nowhere to easily land. A small channel on Cree's southeast side is rich with intertidal life. Seals are frequently seen between Cree and Austin Islands. Cree used to be a lookout where First Nations watched for enemies and whales.

AUSTIN AND BAUKE ISLANDS

The southeast side of Bauke Island was logged a long time ago. Landing on the beach on the east side of Bauke is possible at high tide. Austin and Bauke Islands have short walking trails. There are outstanding tidepools to explore between Austin and Effingham, and two sea caves can be found on the south shore of Austin Island

Before the introduction of modern navigation instruments such as GPS, ship captains would mistaken Barkley Sound for the entrance of Juan de Fuca Strait. Ship crews often realized their horrific mistake too late — once they hit the rugged shores of west Vancouver Island.

But even technological advance is no assurance of safety, for Austin has been the site of several shipwrecks. One famous wreck occurred on March

Wreck of the Vanlene, *1972. Copyright PRNPR Archives*

14, 1972, when a giant freighter, the *Vanlene*, ran aground near Austin Island. The ship was carrying 300 Dodge Colt automobiles en route to Vancouver from Japan.

The crew members (from Honk Kong) all survived, but they were not able to save the ship. They sent out a Mayday call erroneously reporting they were off the coast of Washington state. Search-and-rescue teams took a long time to find the *Vanlene* due to the wildly inaccurate position report. The vessel was finally located, but despite the involvement of several rescue vessels the *Vanlene* could not be saved. Her captain had apparently lost his way, and investigators found that all navigation instruments on the ageing vessel were non-functioning. The captain had navigated across the Pacific with just an ordinary compass!

Helicopter airlifting cars from the Vanlene *wreck, 1972. Copyright Parks Canada*

The wreck of the *Vanlene* caused a major oil spill and the federal government was unprepared for such a catastrophe in its brand new national park. A boom was hastily strung together to contain the leaked oil. More oil was pumped directly from the *Vanlene*, and Mother Nature helped dissipate the rest. Nearly half the cars were salvaged from the sinking vessel by helicopter. Some years later, west coast storms broke the vessel in two and the *Vanlene* settled deeper and disappeared from sight. The wreck used to be a tourist attraction and is still visited by divers. Salt water corrosion ate away at the ship and its cargo of metal cars, but the rubber bits and pieces occasionally floated to the surface. Twenty-six tires were found on Clarke Island on one day.

Sea arch on Effingham Island. Copyright Parks Canada

EFFINGHAM, GILBERT AND RAYMOND ISLANDS

Effingham Island was originally called Village Island because there was a large First Nations village on the island, located where the reserve is today. The name was changed to Effingham in 1905. There was a secondary village site in Effingham Bay which may have been used as a trading post. The bay's large size and sheltered position near the Gilbert Island trading post made the Effingham Bay an important anchorage for trading schooners (McMillan and St.Claire, 2003:21). A fishing station was also established on the island by the Anderson Company in about 1866 (Peterson, 1999:104).

Permission must be obtained prior to landing at or walking through the Indian Reserve. A 15-minute trail connects the reserve to Effingham Bay, which is a popular, sheltered overnight anchorage for sailing yachts and motorboats. The bay has two gravel beaches where kayakers can land. A canoe run can also be found in the small bay on the northwest tip of Effingham. Hiking to the lake on the island is very difficult and people often get lost trying to do so. If you get there, you may find one species of fish in the lake: stickleback.

There is evidence of a structure on the southeast side of Effingham Bay that might possibly have been the winter quarters of Captain John Meares. Meares explored the area in 1788, one year after Captain Charles Barkley. Meares' name was given to the steep bluff (Meares Bluff) on the southeast

Wreck of the Tuscan Prince. *Copyright Parks Canada*

side of Effingham Island. The bluff is approximately 100 m high and hosts an impressive eagle's nest. It is possible that Meares Bluff could have been used as a fortress site by First Nations. The steep cliffs on the south shore of the island are the location of several shipwrecks, including the *Tuscan Prince* (1923), the *Tutsana* (1924), and the *Salmon King* (1976).

Paddling Effingham's shoreline is spectacular. Sea arches and caves grace the east and north shore. It's possible to paddle through the sea arch south of the Indian Reserve when the tide is high and the sea calm. Otherwise you will have to deal with the swell in the tunnel, which can be challenging and even dangerous for novice paddlers.

There are many culturally modified trees on Effingham, as well as near the campsite on Gilbert Island. Gilbert's campsite faces north and is rather shady. This campsite and the one on Benson are the least crowded because only intermediate and advanced paddlers visit these outer islands. The area around the campsite on Gilbert was previously logged. A trail leads from the campsite to a south-facing cove, a good spot to collect driftwood. A unique aspect of the beach on Gilbert is its reddish-brown sand.

The sandy beach on Raymond Island is a nice spot to sunbathe or have lunch. A low to medium tide is recommended for landing on the beach. The wreck of the *Maria J. Smith*, which went down in 1869, lies south of Raymond Island.

Paddling in northwest Barkley Sound

The area of Barkley Sound north of Forbes Island and Lyall Point is commonly called the "Toquart Bay area," even though Toquart Bay proper is just a small part of this area. Northwest Barkley Sound is the traditional territory of the Toquaht First Nation. Toquaht means "people of the narrow channel."

The Toquaht First Nation almost disappeared in the 1930s and their numbers are still very low (just over 100 individuals). The Toquaht today live primarily in Ucluelet, though three dozen live on Macoah Reserve, with its long, sand-and-gravel beach spreading along the shore.

The Maa-nulth First Nations' Final Agreement was adopted in November 2007 by five aboriginal groups including the Toquaht First Nations, and by the governments of British Columbia and Canada. Under this agreement, the land package for the Toquaht First Nations includes 196 hectares of former Indian Reserves and 1293 hectares of additional lands. Most of these additional lands, yet to be given back, are located around the shoreline of Toquart Bay and include the follow islands: Bazett Island, Bryant Islands, Castle Island, Curwen Island, David Island, Forbes Island, Larkins Island, Ottaway Islet, Page Island, Pinder Island, Rowlands Islet, Refuge Island, Spilling Islet and St. Ines Island. Stopper Islands are not included in the land package.At this point, it is unknown what will happen with the access for kayakers to the land that will be given back to Toquaht First Nations.

Apart from the "traditional" First Nations reserves, much of the land in the Toquart Bay area is Crown land, on which it is legal and usually free for individuals to camp. Commercial operators, however, are required to have a license to use Crown land for their business activities. In Canada, most beaches along the coast (even beaches adjacent to private land) are public property and paddlers can legally stop there. "Beach" refers to the area from the intertidal zone up to the higher high water mark.

Northwest Barkley Sound is a great place for paddlers, especially in the spring (March and April), when the herring and their spawn attract sea lions and whales. Sea lions feed on the herring and whales on herring eggs.

Bear watching along the shoreline of Vancouver Island in the Toquart Bay area is good April to November with best viewing in the mornings and evenings during low tide. Bears feed on crabs hidden beneath rocks along the shoreline. Crabs are not only a delicacy for humans but also for bears. Bears can also be seen fishing along salmon spawning creeks during the fall and when using the shoreline for traveling.

PIPESTEM INLET

This beautiful area, surrounded by mountains over 1,000 m high, is rarely visited by kayakers. A trading post was located on Hillier Island in the 1850s. Circumnavigation of Hillier Island is only possible at high tide. Nearby Lucky Creek was once the site of a fish cannery. At high tide it is possible to paddle upstream far enough to see the Lucky Creek waterfall, which is spectacular during the winter or after several days of rain. A short trail nearby leads to the top of the falls.

Pipestem is known for its warm waters. Surface water temperature can reach above 22 °C (70°F). Paddlers will encounter a few shellfish farms

and cabins along the inlet. There are two small campsites in the inlet. The one near the mouth is located at Cataract Creek, which is also a great spot to collect oysters at low tide. This campsite should be avoided during the fall when the spawning salmon attract many bears. The second campsite is a sandy beach located at the far end of the inlet.

Sea arch on Bryant Islands.
Photos: JF Marleau

STOPPER, ST. INES, SNOWDEN, BRYANT AND DAVID ISLANDS

Toquart River, with its small waterfalls, lies north of Snowden Island. It's a nice place for birding, especially during winter months. Snowden Island, formerly Image Island, was glorious before it was logged. A survey made prior to logging noted over 100 culturally modified trees, several of which had had planks removed. Snowden has no beach; the best landing place in a small bay on the southeast side.

Double kayaks are faster and more stable than single kayaks. Photo: JF Marleau

There is a wilderness campsite north of the Macoah Reserve that can be reached from the Toquart Bay Road via an old logging road. This campsite is small, with room for only a few tents, but it has a sandy beach and an outhouse.

The Stopper Islands are forested with old growth trees. There are two campsites on the islands, each suitable for a few tents. One is located on the southern Stopper Island, facing several small islands in the passage between the two Stoppers. Access to the small gravel beach is easy at high or low tide but difficult at medium tide. The other campsite is on the southeast tip of the southern Stopper Island. Landing on this beach is good during any tide. There are a few culturally modified trees behind this campsite. An oyster farm was set up on the north side of the northern island in 2003, and two herring fish pens were established near the Stoppers Islands in 2005.

The fish pens near the Stoppers Islands are used in the spring by Toquaht First Nations to release live spawning herring captured by seine fishing boat. Kelp blades are placed inside the fish pens for the herring to lay their eggs on. First Nations salt the herring roe (eggs on kelp) during the harvest and ship them mostly to the Japanese market where herring roe is considered a delicacy. The herring will later be released back to sea. Harvesting herring roe is a traditional activity for First Nations. Traditionally, hemlock branches were used so the fish could lay their eggs on them.

St. Ines Island was logged in the early 1960s and then reforested. Logging cables are still visible on this island. A decent campsite with enough space for ten tents is located on the north side. Beach access is good at medium to high tides, but is difficult at low tide. There's a sea cave on the southwest side of St. Ines and First Nations canoe runs near the campsite.

The Bryant Islands are rarely visited but are very interesting to paddle around. When the sea state is calm, kayakers can paddle through a big arch filled with colorful intertidal life. The channel within the arch leads to a very secluded beach. There is room to erect a tent or two on the Bryant Islands.

David Island is a well-kept paddler's secret. This island has two beautiful sandy beaches. The north side of David Island is suitable for up to 3 small tents when the night tides are not extremely high. Access to the north beach is better at medium or high tide, while the sheltered beach on the south side is only accessible at low or medium tides. A seal colony inhabits the west side of David Island and the south side of Ottaway Island.

MAYNE BAY

Mayne Bay supports a seal colony in the Shears Islands, which are rarely visited by kayakers. Nearby, secluded Entrance Inlet is home to aquaculture farms and floating cabins. Gravel and sandy beaches dot the south shore of Mayne Bay.

In 2003, Mayne Bay played a role in a bizarre ship sinking. The 42-m, rusted-out ship *Black Dragon* had arrived on B.C.'s west coast four years earlier, as did three other ships, all packed with illegal immigrants from China. The *Black Dragon*'s Korean crew dumped the migrants on an inhabited island in the Queen Charlotte Islands and raced back toward international waters. They were intercepted by a Canadian Coast Guard patrol vessel and the *Black Dragon* was seized. The crew members were acquitted in B.C. Supreme Court.

It was sold to the Port Alberni Artificial Reef Society until being resold for one dollar to two brothers from Nanaimo. To avoid paying moorage, the new owners tied the ship (without authorization) to the Department of National Defence buoy in south Mayne Bay. No government agency wanted to take responsibility for this white elephant, and the buck passed back and forth for five months until, on October 2, 2003, the *Black Dragon* sank in 40 m of water during a winter storm. When the wreck began leaking diesel fuel right next door to a national park, suddenly the matter became urgent. Attempts were made to salvage the hulk, but it was mired some 6 m deep in the mud bottom and resisted all attempts to raise it.

With redoubled effort it was floated at last, and placed under tow on its final voyage to a salvage yard in Ladysmith. But the uncooperative *Black Dragon* got the last laugh by sinking again, unexpectedly, near Sidney. Vexed officials decided to leave it where it was, and thus ended the saga.

PINKERTON ISLANDS

When you paddle through the beautiful Pinkerton Islands (formerly named Hundred Islands) it is hard to understand why they were not included in the national park, whose boundary almost touches the outermost island of the group. The Pinkertons' sheltered waters offer many short, beautiful routes to explore. It is a peaceful place where you can paddle close to shore with the forest canopy draped on both sides of your kayak.

The islands were named after James Pinkerton, who homesteaded there in the 1890s. The Pinkertons have no campsites, but there are a few private cabins. Equis Beach, to the north, is a First Nations reserve. The beach is very good for clam digging and the Tseshaht have a commercial shellfish licence for this location.

SALMON BEACH RESORT

Salmon Beach Resort, located on the west side of Loudoun Channel, looks like a town when viewed from the BGI. Salmon Beach Resort can be reached by boat or by driving the Barkley Main logging road from Ucluelet or Toquart Bay. In the late 1800s, the provincial government wanted to develop a town at this location, but the oceanfront lacked shelter for a good harbour.

Until 1992 the site was a seasonal recreational village where only RVs and trailers were allowed, no permanent structures, and occupancy was limited to no more than 180 days per year. Nowadays, properties are being sold and cabins being built, though there is still no running water and there are issues regarding sewage disposal. The small community is administered by the Salmon Beach Owners Association and the Alberni-Clayoquot Regional District.

A long sandy beach on the north side of Salmon Beach Resort offers good opportunities for exploring on foot. When seas are greater than 2.5 m it is also a good spot for surfing.

Deer are abundant in the BGI. Photo: Wendy Szaniszlo

Terrestrial Animals

The Broken Group contains a wide diversity of wildlife habitat, including sheltered and exposed saltwater coastline, forest, bog, freshwater systems, and an intertidal zone of mud, sand and gravel beach. Each of these habitats is home to a host of plants and animals uniquely adapted to survive in its particular conditions. Critters of all kinds inhabit the islands — small, large, furry and slimy. All are wild and are an integral part of Pacific Rim National Park Reserve.

Racoon: B. Schramm

Terrestrial animals a kayaker might see include the mouse, garter snake (_not_ a venomous species), red squirrel, mink, deer, racoon, river otter, wolf, black bear and banana slug. There are no grizzly bears on Vancouver Island, but black bears are common on the west coast. A black bear was reported in the BGI for the first time in the summer of 2005. Cougars are far more elusive. There have only been two reports (unconfirmed) of cougars in the BGI, both in 2002. Only slugs and wolves will be discussed in this section.

BANANA SLUGS

The banana slug is the second largest slug species in the world, after the European grey slug. They are fascinating little critters. Ugly and unappealing at first, these slimy animals will grow on you (well, *stick* on you, to be precise). Banana slugs can grow to a length of 25 centimetres. They get their name from their coloration, for they come in any colour a banana can — unripe green, yellow, sometimes yellow with dark spots, or rotten dark brown.

Banana slug. Photo: Mary Watson

They don't taste like a banana though! In fact, if you lick a slug you'll be in for a surprise — your tongue will go numb. Slug slime contains a natural anaesthetic that functions to protect the animal from predators.

A sprinting slug can scramble 60 cm in 43 seconds, riding on a trail of slime. This is many times its own body length. If you think of slugs as slow, try lying on your belly with your hands clasped behind you and your knees bent, and then wriggle your way along. How many body lengths can you do in 43 seconds?

Slugs are hermaphrodites, possessing both male and female sex organs. Individuals can copulate with themselves if mates are scarce, or attract a partner. The banana slug also gives a whole new twist to the adage "bigger is better." Slugs have a large penis — so large, in fact, that they will actually get stuck together during copulation, occasionally making it a challenge to disengage. When that happens, the only way they can separate is for one of them to chew the male apparatus off. The amputee will be able to function only as a female for the rest of its life. Biologists actually have a term for this deed: apophallation.

Banana slugs play an important role in the ecosystem. They are recyclers, chewing organic matter with their radula (a specialized tongue with 27,000 teeth) and turning it into compost, which then gives forest seedlings a healthy start. Slugs live up to seven years.

Wolf on Willis Island. Photo: Doug Andrew

WOLVES

The coastal wolf, weighing up to 45 kg, is smaller than other wolves found in Canada. Its fur is usually reddish grey. An estimated 200 wolves inhabit Vancouver Island, though the population fluctuates depending on habitat quality and the availability of prey. Coastal wolves feed mainly on deer, but also dine on bear, spawning salmon, dead marine mammals and smaller mammals such as river otter, mink and raccoon. In 2003, a wolf pack fed on a dead whale in Gibraltar Island lagoon.

Wolves can live up to ten years in the wild and reach maturity at two years of age. They are social and territorial animals. Only the alpha male and female are allowed to breed within a pack. Reproduction of the other pack members is suppressed by the dominant pair. These non-breeding individuals help raise the pups.

Wolves are transient visitors in the BGI. They have been consistently hunting and denning on the islands since 2001. Strong swimmers, wolves came to the BGI in search of food, and it is expected that they will stay as long as there is food to sustain them. Before they moved into the archipelago there was an abundance of Columbia black-tailed deer, a small species related to the mule deer. For the newly arrived wolves it was an all-you-can-eat buffet! The islands had been intensively grazed by the deer, and wolves will affect the ecosystem by diminishing the deer population.

Frequent wolf sightings were reported in the BGI in 2001. By the following year the population was estimated at three individuals. In 2003, the wolves formed a pack and had three pups on Gibraltar, though one was found dead on Turtle Island in September. In 2004 the pack comprised four or five adult wolves, and produced four pups on Effingham Island.

Parks Canada puts much time and effort into ensuring that wolves and humans can coexist in the BGI. They do this by monitoring the wolf population and hazing wolves that exhibit unnatural behaviour — that is, behaviour indicating they are too comfortable around humans. In the past, negligent or ignorant people actively fed the wolves, which naturally learned to associate food with humans. In 2004, BGI wardens were forced to destroy a wolf when the food-conditioned animal was observed stealing food and chewing on cookware and tents. This wolf no longer feared humans and had become a safety issue. The animal weighed only 28 kg, indicating it may have been starving.

In 2000, a wolf severely injured a sleeping camper in Clayoquot Sound and the entire pack was destroyed by provincial conservation officers. These wolves had also been fed and photographed by recreational kayakers. When wild carnivores lose their fear of humans and learn to expect human food, they become a public safety risk. These "problem animals" are often destroyed. They pay the price for human negligence with their lives.

A wolf can smell food to up to two km away. If you have food in your tent and wolves are in the vicinity, they will know. Wolves have been known to "inspect" campsites in the BGI during the night. It is very important to keep your campsite and kitchen very clean, and your food, garbage and other wildlife attractants stored securely in the hatches of your kayak. Make sure the hatches are secured. Do not keep food in your tent. Negligent campers can be charged under the Canada National Parks Act by park wardens.

It is equally important to teach wolves that it is not acceptable to approach you or your campsite. A good wolf is a scared wolf, when it comes to human interaction. If you encounter a wolf, don't run! That just makes it think you might be food worth pursuing, and a wolf can run much faster than you — up to 70 km per hour. Instead, show the wolf you are dominant and dangerous: make yourself look bigger; make noise (use your whistle); be aggressive; wave sticks or your paddle; throw rocks. Keep your group together and pick children up in your arms. Use pepper spray if the wolf approaches closely and is aggressive. In the rare case of an attack, fight back. Hit the eyes or nose of the wolf, as they are very sensitive.

Always keep a distance of at least 100 m from wolves. Avoid den sites and closed areas. Pups can be very curious and adults are normally not too far away. If you encounter pups, leave immediately. Wolves have only shown aggression toward humans in the BGI on a few occasions, and no one has been injured. Usually this has occurred when kayakers approached too close to pups or a den. A defensive reaction is normal in this situation. The co-existence of wolves and humans in the BGI is possible if visitors take the responsibility to help keep wolves wild.

Please report any wolf, cougar or bear sighting or kills to park wardens at 250-726-8175.

Researchers identify individual humpback whales by comparing the unique colours and markings on the underside of their tails. Photo: Wendy Szaniszlo

Marine Mammals

Marine mammal viewing, particularly of whales and sea lions, is very popular in the BGI. This section provides useful information pertaining to gray whales, humpback whales, orcas, sea otters, harbour seals and sea lions.

WHALES

Whales are common in and around the BGI. They are charismatic and create excitement for west coast visitors. Whales are marine  mammals and belong to the family *Cetacea*. Biologists divide them into two groups: toothed whales and baleen whales. Toothed whales feed on fish, mammals and squid. Baleen whales use their broom-like baleen to filter tiny organisms from the water. All whales have a thick layer of insulating blubber to keep them warm. Like all other mammals they have warm blood, breathe air, give birth to live young, have mammary glands and even have a few hairs. Whales communicate with complex underwater vocalizations. When searching for whales, watch for their "spout" — a spray of mist a few metres high — and listen for the *whoosh* when they exhale at the surface.

Commercial whaling was practiced on Vancouver Island until 1967. Today, Japan, Norway and Iceland still engage in whaling. Some aboriginal groups in Alaska, Siberia, the Canadian Arctic and Washington state practice traditional subsistence whaling.

GRAY WHALES

Gray whales grow to a length of 15 metres (49 ft) and weigh up to 36 tonnes. They may live up to 60 years. Their skin is mottled and encrusted with barnacles and whale lice. The mottling creates distinctive markings on each whale that researchers use to identify individuals. Gray whales don't have a dorsal fin but rather have a set of knuckle-like ridges.

Gray whales typically blow three to five times before diving, and stay under for an average of five minutes. On its final breath, a gray whale will usually arch its back and sometimes show its tail as it dives. It is uncommon to see gray whales breaching (jumping out of the water) or spyhopping (poking their head out of the water to look around).

Gray whales usually feed in shallow waters (under 20 m) and within 3 km of shore. They feed on tiny little critters in the water column and in the bottom sediment. In Barkley Sound, grays feed primarily on mysids (tiny, shrimp-like animals) and amphipods that swarm in carpets just above the sea bottom, usually near kelp fields. Grays also feed on sandy and muddy bottoms. They gulp in a mouthful of sediment and then push their massive tongue (up to one tonne in size!) up against the roof of their mouth, squeezing water and sediment out through the baleen and leaving the yummy invertebrates behind. Each spring, gray whales feed on herring eggs in the

Breaching gray whale. Photo: Wendy Szaniszlo

Toquart Bay area. One of the largest animals on earth, gray whales feed on some of the tiniest animals. They consume about a tonne of food per day!

Gray whales spend their winters in Baja, Mexico, where they breed and give birth in warm, sheltered lagoons. Females give birth to a single calf weighing one tonne and measuring 5 m long. Calves are born in January after a 12-month gestation period. They feed on fat-rich milk and gain 25 kg per day.

The whales leave Baja between mid-February and April to start their northern migration to the summer feeding grounds in the Alaska's Bering Sea — an 8,000-km voyage, one of the longest known migrations of any mammal. During their northern migration, gray whales travel near shore. March and April are the best months to see gray whales in Barkley Sound. Not all gray whales migrate to Alaska. Approximately 75 to 100 individuals spend the summer feeding along the west coast of Vancouver Island, the so-called "resident" whales. Many residents are recognized and nicknamed by local whale watchers. In the fall, gray whales head offshore to embark on their southern migration back to Mexico.

Gray whales were hunted almost to extinction, and were given international protection in 1947. The population rose from a mere 250 individuals in 1947 to a population today of approximately 18,000. This recovery is one of the most successful of all whale species. The Atlantic gray whale population has not been so lucky: They were hunted to extinction.

Breaching humpback whale calf. Photo: Wendy Szaniszlo

HUMPBACK WHALES

Humpback whales were intensely hunted in B.C. at the turn of the century but are slowly recovering. There were approximately 1,000 humpbacks in the North Pacific when the species was protected in the 1960s. Since then the population has increased substantially, but humpbacks are still designated as a threatened species in Canada. Humpback whales were commonly seen in Barkley Sound during the summers of 2005, 2006 and 2007.

Humpbacks are up to 18 m (59 ft) in length and weigh up to 41 tonnes. This species has distinctive identifying features. It is dark above and lighter underneath, with very long pectoral flippers and a unique hump in front of its small, triangular dorsal fin. The distinctive black and white patterns on the underside of the fluke allow researchers to identify individuals.

Humpback whales are the most acrobatic baleen whale and are known to frequently breach. Their blows are taller than those of gray whales. Humpbacks normally breathe a few times and then dive for five to 12 minutes. They can hold their breath for about 20 minutes.

Humpback whales feed on small schooling fish such as herring, pilchard (sardines) and sandlance. When in larger groups they frequently feed co-operatively using a technique called "bubble net feeding." By exhaling air underwater, the humpbacks create a screen of bubbles encircling a school of fish. The whales then dive below the school and lunge to the surface, together, mouths wide open. This behaviour is called "lunge feeding" and humpbacks employ this method whether they feed individually or as a group.

Orcas or killer whales. Photo: JF Marleau

ORCAS

Orcas are sometimes referred to as killer whales. *Orca* means "demon from hell" in Latin — testimony, no doubt, to this whale's mouthful of impressive teeth. Orcas are distributed throughout all the world's oceans, including the Arctic and Antarctic. Approximately 725 killer whales live in the Pacific Northwest between Alaska and British Columbia. Males can live up to 50 years and females up to 80 years. Until 1980, killer whales were harvested for meat and oil (Harbo, 2000:184).

Killer whales are black on top and white below and have a large, distinctive dorsal fin, standing in males up to 1.8 m (6 ft) tall. Researchers use the shape of the dorsal fin and the white "saddle patch" behind it to identify individual whales. Males are larger than females and can be up to 10 metres (33 ft) long and weigh 7.2 tons. Killer whales can dive to depths of over 1,000 m.

There are three distinct groups of orca whales: resident, transient and offshore. Resident orcas travel in large groups (called pods) and feed on fish. There are about 305 resident orcas in the Pacific Northwest (Harbo, 2000:183), though they are rarely seen in Barkley Sound.

Transient orcas feed primarily on marine mammals such as seals, sea lions, sea otters, porpoises and other whales. They have even been observed to take the odd deer or bird. Transients travel in small pods of five individuals or less. The dorsal fins of transients are usually more pointed than those of resident killer whales. Transients can occasionally be seen travelling and

An orca near a few tasty sea lions. Copyright Parks Canada

feeding in Barkley Sound but it is very difficult to predict their movements. Surprisingly, orcas are rarely observed between Wouwer and Batley Islands where there is a high concentration of sea lions.

Little is known about offshore orcas because they are seen so rarely. They are physiologically and genetically different from the other orcas. Offshores are smaller, and have rounder dorsal fins and different saddle patch patterns than the other subspecies.

SEA OTTERS

Thick, luxurious sea otter fur was discovered during Captain Cook's expedition in Nootka Sound in 1778. A very lucrative business soon began and many traders came to the coast. The British and Spanish traded iron, alcohol, tools, and gunpowder with First Nations in exchange for sea otter pelts. Captain Cook himself sold sea otter fur in China for an amount equivalent to several thousand Canadian dollars per pelt today. Demand for its fur was so high that, just 30 years after European contact, the sea otter was almost extinct.

The last known sea otter in Canadian waters was killed in the Queen Charlotte Islands in the 1920s. Between 1969 and 1972, sea otters from Alaska were reintroduced to the Bunsby Islands, south of Brooks Peninsula on northwest Vancouver Island. They took to their new home, and the sea

Sea otter wrapped in kelp. Photo: Wendy Szaniszlo

otter population in B.C. is currently over 3,000 individuals. The population off west coast Vancouver Island is increasing by 2% annually. Male sea otters usually colonize new territories first, and females later move in. In 2004 about eight sea otters were spotted in Barkley Sound, and this number is expected to increase.

Sea otters are the only marine mammals that do not have a layer of fat to keep them warm. Instead, sea otters have incredibly dense fur — the densest of any mammal with up to a million hairs per square inch in some areas. The fur traps air next to the skin, keeping the otter warm. To maintain its insulating properties, sea otters must constantly groom themselves and keep themselves clean.

Sea otters also have a very high metabolic rate. They consume one-third of their body weight in food every day, mainly sea urchins, abalone, sea stars, clams, mussels and crabs. Seas otters dive up to 100 m (333 ft) and remain underwater for up 5 minutes to harvest food. They float on their back when they eat and frequently use a rock to crack the shells of their prey. The major predators of sea otters are orcas and poachers.

Sea otters are often confused with river otters. River otters are common in the BGI and are seen in streams, in the ocean and on shore. Sea otters spend almost all their life in the ocean and rarely go ashore. Sea otters are found in more exposed waters while river otters favour sheltered waters. The two species look different as well. Sea otters have a small tail, whereas river otter tails are long. Sea otters are also larger and heavier than their river cousins, growing up to 1.5 m (5 ft) in length and weighing up to 39 kg (86 lb). Sea otters' colour varies from brown to black. Their life expectancy is 15 years.

Kelp beds are important habitat for sea otters. They wrap themselves in kelp fronds to anchor themselves when resting or sleeping. Sea otters are the chief natural predator of sea urchins, which feed on kelp. With the slaughter of sea otters during the fur trade, the urchin population shot up, which in turn decimated the kelp habitat, leaving behind what biologists call "urchin barrens." As sea otter populations return to historical levels, this ecosystem imbalance could correct itself.

Harbour seals. Photo: Wendy Szaniszlo

HARBOUR SEALS

Harbour seals are abundant in Barkley Sound; there about 20 areas where they haul out. These seals can be 1.8 m (6 ft) long and weigh up to 102 kg (225 lb). They are a mottled black, white, and brown in colour. Like all true seals, harbour seals have small front flippers and no external ears. Harbour seals are quiet and curious, and are very sensitive to disturbance. Kayakers should stay at least 100 m from seal haulouts. When seals are distressed they rapidly move into the water. Seals feed on fish and are the primary source of food for transient killer whales in Barkley Sound.

California sea lions. Photo: Wendy Szaniszlo

SEA LIONS

The sea lions in Barkley Sound are the larger, noisier cousin of the harbour seal. Think of sea lions as bears with flippers. When swimming, sea lions usually dive forward and show their backs, whereas harbour seals usually only show their heads and quietly duck under the water. Sea lions are large carnivores with enormous front flippers that can be rotated underneath their bodies to "stand" and "walk" on shore. In the water these flippers propel the animal with speed and agility. Sea lions command respect due to their size, strength and speed. On occasion, a few sea lions have been reported as being aggressive toward surfers in the Long Beach unit of the national park. Keep a safe distance.

Sea lions haul out on and around Wouwer and Batley Islands. They can be seen regularly from August and into the fall. Over 2,400 sea lions were recorded here in October, 2004. It is common to see sea lions feeding on schools of fish. The water frequently boils with tiny prey fish as they try to escape predators such as sea lions and humpback whales.

Two species of sea lions inhabit the Broken Group Islands: California sea lions and Steller sea lions. California sea lions are more abundant in the fall. They are a dark chocolate brown colour and have a loud honking bark. Mature males have a blond bump on their forehead and can weigh up to

Steller sea lions. Photo: Wendy Szaniszlo

365 kg. Only male California sea lions migrate north to B.C., departing for the southern breeding grounds in May and return in early August. Females and pups stay year round in California.

Steller sea lion bulls are much larger than the Californias and can weigh up to 1000 kg. They are blonde-brown in colour and their vocalization is more like a roar or growl. Stellers of all ages and both sexes can be seen in Barkley Sound. Park waters are considered haulouts and not rookeries (the latter being where sea lions breed and have pups), therefore young animals are usually pups that were not born in the national park. Steller sea lions are listed as a Species of Special Concern in Canada. The population of Steller sea lions has plummeted in western Alaska over the past few decades.

Sea lions used to be hunted until 1970. Even the Royal Canadian Air Force used to drop bombs on sea lion rookeries and haulouts for target practice. Sea lions are now protected under the Canada Fisheries Act, and those in the national park have additional protection under the Canada National Park Act. Although attitudes toward sea lions have changed somewhat, many fishers still consider them pests.

Sea lions today are the focus of much study, and are considered an indicator of fishery abundance and ecosystem health. Sea lions are very intelligent and have good memory. The U.S. Navy uses California sea lions to guard and protect military facilities and ships from underwater threats.

Bald eagle feeding on a dead sea lion. Photo: JF Marleau

Birds

Two hundred and forty-seven species of birds can be seen in Pacific Rim National Park Reserve. Barkley Sound is a major congregation and breeding site for numerous bird species, including some threatened species.

Some of the more common species during the summer are the cormorant, oyster catcher, great blue heron, belted kingfisher, marbled murrelet, common murre, rufous humming bird, bald eagle, raven and northwestern crow.

The northwestern crow is very abundant in the BGI and extremely intelligent. This species is an expert in stealing food, especially at campsites. As soon as you turn your back they will be after your munchies, tenaciously attempting to open plastic containers, food bags and even kayak hatches. Crows can be noisy and bothersome —sometimes they even harass bald eagles. The best way to get rid of them is to make sure they don't have access to food. Store all foodstuff securely and don't leave your kitchen area unattended.

Crows naturally feed on intertidal organisms and other birds' eggs. Sometimes crows drop clams on rocks from on high to break open their shells.

Ravens and crows are often mistaken for each other. They have three major differences:

1) Raven tails have a triangular profile, while crow tails are rectangular.

2) Ravens are larger than crows.

3) Ravens have a diverse repertoire of calls and can imitate the sound of the crow. Crows have fewer calls.

Above: northwestern crow

Right: bald eagle peaking out of his perch in a cedar tree.
Photos: B. Schramm

BALD EAGLE

Barkley Sound has one of the highest densities of bald eagles in North America. Most bald eagles leave the BGI in the fall to follow migrating salmon up spawning streams.

They return to the coast in mid-February. Bald eagles are plentiful in the islands during spring and summer. There are so many eagles, in fact, that by your third day in the BGI you'll pay no more attention to them.

Bald eagles stand 1 m (3 ft) tall and have an impressive wingspan of 2 m (6 ft). Females are larger than males and can weigh up to 7 kg (15 lb). An eagle's bones are hollow and weigh less than half the total weight of its feathers (Gordon, 1994:18). The chicks grow quickly; by the time they first attempt to fly they are the same size or bigger than their parents. As the immature eagle moults each year, its feathers are replaced with progressively shorter ones (Gordon, 1994:17). An immature bald eagle (less than four years of age) has a brown head and tail. It looks much like a golden eagle, but the latter are rare in Barkley Sound.

Bald eagles reach sexual maturity at five years of age and can live for 50 years in captivity (though likely much less in the wild). Bald eagle pairs usually stay together for life and share chick rearing activities. Bald eagles have vision seven times more acute than humans to help them find their prey, and powerful hooked beaks and sharp talons to grab it.

Eagle nest on a small island.
Photo: B. Schramm

Bald eagles feed mainly on fish. They also hunt gulls, water-fowl and small mammals, though they are also scaven-gers and will steal food when they get the opportunity. Benjamin Franklin, who fa-voured the wild turkey over the eagle for the United States national symbol, said of the eagle: "It is a bird of bad moral character. He doesn't get his living honestly" (Gordon, 1994:20). Despite these com-ments, the majestic bald eagle is a beautiful creature to watch. It is common to see bald eagles plunging toward the water to seize a fish swimming close to the surface.

Bald eagles defend their territory against intruders. Their territories can be up to 800 m in all directions from their nest. Bald eagle pairs usually keep the same nest and increase the nest size year after

Bald eagle catching a fish. JF Marleau

year. A bald eagle nest can be 3 m (10 ft) wide and 1 m (3 ft) deep and weigh 1 tonne — the equivalent in size and weight to an upside-down Volkswagen bug. One nest found on Bonilla Island, on the north coast of B.C., measured 6.6 m across and 4.8 m deep (Obee, 1998:34). The size of a nest is limited by the strength of the tree; storms and decay dictate its longevity.

The nest is built in the crown of a tree, usually located along the shoreline so the eagles can scan for food and protect their nest simultaneously. The inside is lined with soft mosses and plants to protect and insulate the eggs and chicks. Bald eagles usually lay two eggs, but can lay one or three. The chick mortality rate is very high.

The BGI is a great place for tidepooling. Photo: Jacqueline Windh

Intertidal Life

Photo: B. Schramm

The intertidal zone is the area on the beach that is covered and uncovered by the tide each day. The BGI has an incredible diversity of intertidal life, including sea stars, shellfish, sea cucumbers, sea anemones, moonsnails and sea urchins. It would take a dozen volumes to provide in-depth information on all the intertidal organisms you will see, but some of the more common species are described below. Most intertidal organisms live in the low intertidal zone — the area covered by water most of the time. This zone is prime habitat because the water provides food, oxygen and washes away wastes. The best time to explore tidepools is at low tide.

The intertidal zone is fragile. Its denizens are small, soft-bodied or thin-shelled, and vulnerable. Avoid stepping on animals and plants and gently return any overturned rocks to their original position. Fill in any holes you dig. Remember that it is unlawful to remove any natural objects from a national park. This includes taking even ONE shell. Shells are homes to smaller animals like crabs and also supply beach ecosystems with calcium. If every one of the thousands of annual visitors took just one shell, many hermit crabs would be rendered homeless. Take photographs, sketches and memories instead.

Rocky intertidal areas are slippery. Be safe and aware! Large waves can unexpectedly crash ashore, even on an otherwise calm day, and wash you away. Intertidal animals have adaptations to remain attached to rocks. You don't. Always keep an eye out for waves and never enter surge channels!

SEA STARS

Sea stars are commonly called starfish but they are not fish at all. The Pacific Northwest is home to a variety of sea stars, 36 of which are found in British Columbia waters. None of the BGI sea stars are poisonous or bite. Most of the sea stars described here feed on barnacles, clams, mussels or oysters. The larger sea stars, such as the sunflower star, also prey on bigger animals like crabs or smaller sea stars.

The manner in which they feed is like something out of a bad science fiction novel. A sea star will use its hundreds of plunger-like feet to wrap around its shellfish prey and slowly pry it open. Once a tiny crack is created, the sea star extrudes its stomach from its mouth opening and inserts it into the mussel. The sea star then digests the mussel within its own shell, after which the sea star retracts its stomach into own body. Predators of sea stars include other sea stars, sea otters and gulls.

The numerous feet on the ventral side of sea stars are controlled by an internal hydraulic system. Sea stars have a water intake/outtake "valve" on the top of their central disc. The hydraulic system controls the movement of each individual foot so the sea star can move.

Sea stars reproduce both sexually and asexually. In the spring females release their eggs, which mix with sperm released by males — the usual method. But a sea star can also reproduce if one of its arms is torn off, with a portion of the central disc still attached to the arm. The torn arm will develop into a new sea star, and the individual that lost its arm will regenerate another. (Please don't test this!)

Sunflower star. Photo: B. Schramm

Leather sea star. Photo: Wendy Szaniszlo

SUNFLOWER STAR

Sunflowers stars are probably the most spectacular of all sea stars. In the BGI they are usually purple, but it is not uncommon to see orange individuals. The body of this species is soft and flexible. They have a broad central disc (or "hub") and 16 to 24 arms, lined on their underside with 15,000 feet. These are the fastest sea stars in this area, able to move up to 110 m (360 ft) in an hour. Their size and speed make them tidepool terrors, initiating flight responses in potential prey.

LEATHER STAR

The leather star has five short, webbed arms. It has a smooth surface and its colour is a variation of brown, grey and rusty red. The leather star exudes a garlic-like smell to deter predators.

BAT STAR

The bat star is often confused with the vermilion and leather stars. Bat stars are common in the BGI. They have five to six webbed arms. Bat stars are rougher to the touch than leather stars and are brilliantly coloured green, red, blue, black or brown.

Bat stars. Photo: JF Marleau

Ochre sea stars. Photo: Wendy Szaniszlo

OCHRE STAR

The ochre star is the most abundant species in rocky intertidal areas. They have five short, thick arms, a rigid body and rough surface. Ochre stars are brown, orange or purple. They can live up to 20 years.

SPINY PINK STAR

The spiny pink sea star can be up to one metre (3 ft) wide. This sea star can be recognized by its large size, pinkish grey colour and 5 long arms. Spiny pink stars are found on soft substrates.

Spiny pink sea star. Photo: JF Marleau

Mottled sea star. Photo: Wendy Szaniszlo

MOTTLED STAR

The mottled star is frequently mistaken for the ochre star, and is in fact appropriately nicknamed the "false ochre star." The mottled star has a smaller disc than the ochre star, as well as narrower, longer arms. Colour is variable from rusty to brown or greyish orange.

SEA ANEMONE

Sea anemones ("a-*nem*-a-nee") look like strange flowers but are actually animals. They are crowned with a ring of fleshy tentacles. There are many species of anemones in BC. They feed by zapping and paralyzing small animals that brush against their tentacles, which are filled with stinging cells. Their stingers are not powerful enough to penetrate human skin. Anemones will close up if you touch them gently. The two most common types of anemones in the BGI are the giant green anemone and the aggregating anemone.

Sea anemone. Photo: JF Marleau

CALIFORNIA SEA CUCUMBER

The California sea cucumber looks like a 50-cm (20-in) long, red cucumber with soft, nipple-like projections. Sea cucumbers have a unique way of protecting themselves. If they sense a predator nearby the cucumber will eviscerate (spit out its digestive tract) to create a diversion while it escapes. This strategy is energetically costly however, because the animal must then regenerate its stomach. Main predators of the sea cucumber are sea stars and fish. Sea cucumbers are bottom feeders. This species is commercially harvested for its strips of muscle, which the Japanese consider a delicacy.

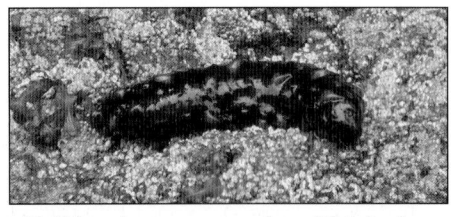

California sea cucumber. JF Marleau

LEWIS'S MOONSNAIL

Moonsnail. Photo: JF Marleau

The moonsnail is a gigantic snail that lives on sandy and muddy bottoms in the low intertidal zone. The snail's extended brown foot is as large as a dinner plate. The moonsnail is able to pull its entire foot into its 12-cm (4.7-in) wide, cream-coloured shell. The animal will suffocate if it stays inside its shell too long.

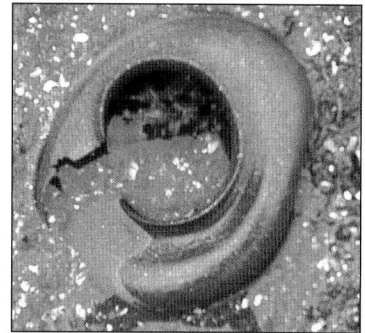

Moonsnail collar. JF Marleau

Moonsnails drill holes into clams with a special, drill-like tongue called a radula. They then excrete an enzyme into the shellfish which liquefies the animal. The moonsnail sucks up the liquid through a straw-like appendage. You may see moonsnail victims on the beach — shells with perfectly round holes near the hinge ligament.

Moonsnails lay eggs in unusual cases. The cases look like grey toilet plungers (without the handle) and have a hole in the top. These egg cases are a mix of eggs, sand and mucus and their shape is moulded by the curvature of the moonsnail's shell. Eggs hatch from the collar in about 6 weeks.

SEA URCHINS

Red sea urchins. B Schramm

Sea urchins are related to sea stars, though they look more like brightly coloured, round pincushions than stars. Their spines help to deter predators. Sea urchins feed on algae and kelp. They chew their food with a unique, toothed jaw holding a set of teeth called an Aristotle's lantern. Predators of urchins include sea stars, fish and sea otters. Sea urchin gonads are a delicacy in Japan.

MUSSELS

Blue mussels. W. Szaniszlo

Two types of mussels are common in the BGI: blue mussels and California mussels. Blue mussels are blue, black or brown in colour and are up to 12.5 cm (5 in) in length. Blue mussels are an introduced species that grow in sheltered locations. California mussels grow to a size of 25 cm (10 in), and are a blend of blue, black, grey, white and purple. Mussels attach themselves to hard surfaces with very strong threads called byssal threads. They live on rocky intertidal areas in large groups. Both species of mussel are delicious but the blue mussel is the type usually served in restaurants. No mussels should be taken in an area with a red tide (PSP) closure.

BARNACLES

Several species of barnacles are found in the BGI. They live in large clusters on rocky shores. The most common one is the small acorn barnacle, found on rocks high in the intertidal zone. Think of barnacles as shrimp living in castles. When in the larvae stage, they drift in the water column seeking a hard surface to attach themselves to. The shrimp-like larva excretes a powerful

Acorn barnacles. W. Szaniszlo

glue from its head and actually attaches itself by sticking its head to a suitable surface it encounters. The barnacle then builds a calcium shell around itself for protection. Barnacles are filter feeders. When the tide covers them they open up their "castle doors" and wave hairy legs (called cirri) back and forth through the water. The cirri snare food particles, which the barnacle pulls back into its castle to eat. When the tides recedes, the barnacle pulls its cirri into its shell and closes its castle door to ensure it does not dry out. Barnacles boast the largest male apparatus of any animal, with a penis up to 20 times the length of its body! This allows them to fertilize several surrounding barnacles.

CRAB

Barkley Sound is home to many crab species. They all have jointed legs, which they use to scuttle sideways. Crabs feed on dead animals, barnacles, worms, clams and mussels. Most crabs, except for the hermit crab, have hard shells for protection. Crabs molt their shells as they outgrow their former ones. They do this by squeezing through a slit in their old shell, discarding it, and hardening their new shell. It common to find intact crab shells on beaches; these shells were most likely molted.

Hermit crabs are different in that they have a soft skeleton with no protective shell. They use the discarded shells from other animals, such as abandoned snail shells, for protection. As the hermit crab grows, it outgrows its shell and needs to get a new one, much like children need new clothes as they grow. This is one reason why not taking shells from beaches is important.

Red rock crabs. Photo: JF Marleau

The number of shells available limits the number of hermit crabs that can survive!

In addition to the hermit crab, two other species you are likely to come across in the Broken Group are the Dungeness crab and the red rock crab. The Dungeness crab is grey-brown in colour and lives in deeper water. The red rock crab (guess what colour this one is!) can frequently be seen along the shore. The red rock crab is usually smaller, up to 20 cm (8 in) wide, with much less meat than the Dungeness (up to 25 cm (10 in) wide). Both species are good to eat, especially the Dungeness which is usually served in restaurants. Know and obey the regulations when harvesting crabs: Don't take females or undersize males.

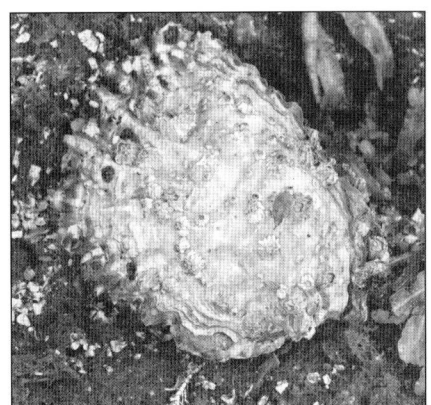

*Japanese Pacific oyster.
Photo: Wendy Szaniszlo*

JAPANESE PACIFIC OYSTER

Japanese Pacific oysters are abundant in the BGI. These oysters grow to 30 cm (12 in) in length and their colour is a whitish grey. The Japanese Pacific oyster was introduced from Japan in the early 1900s. It can live for more than 20 years and can also produce pearls. This species is commercially harvested and very popular in restaurants.

Numerous species of clams can also be found in the BGI. Commercial harvesting is not permitted in the national park.

Kelp

Kelp is an algae, a primitive plant with no vascular system. There are over 100 species of kelp world-wide, of which British Columbia has the greatest diversity in the world. Kelp creates important habitat for fish, sea otters and other organisms. One common species, bull kelp, can grow up to 20 m (66 ft) in length; another common local species, giant kelp, can grow to 30 m (100 ft). Kelp is the fastest growing plant on earth. Under optimal conditions it can grow up to 60 cm (2 ft) per day.

Kelp anchors itself to the sea bottom with holdfasts, a knotted mass that looks like a root ball but in fact doesn't function like the roots of true plants. At the top end of the stalk, a bulb keeps the bull kelp afloat so its blades (leaves) are in the surface sunlight and able to photosynthesize. Bull kelp is an annual plant that grows from March to September and dies off in the winter. Strands and tangled clumps of bull kelp often wash ashore during storms.

Kelp has many uses. First Nations used to make a strong, durable rope out of bull kelp by slathering the stalk with dogfish oil and letting it dry in the sun. They also ate bull kelp blades. Today derivatives from kelp (agar, algin and carrageen) are used in food, pharmaceuticals, cosmetics and a myriad of other products. Kelp is also used in nutritional supplements as well as directly as food. It even plays a part in spa treatments. Kelp farms are common in Asia but there are only a few in B.C. Of the 30 species of kelp in B.C., only six are currently marketed.

Bull kelp. Photo: Wendy Szaniszlo

Left: Giant kelp.
Photo: Wendy Szaniszlo

Bull kelp holdfast. Photo: Wendy Szaniszlo

Trees

The forests of west coast Vancouver Island are predominantly coniferous. Three main species are found here:

- **Western hemlock:** The branches are composed of flat, blunt, short needles of unequal length (5 to 20 mm) arranged irregularly (Pojar and Mackinnon, 1994:30).

Western hemlock needles. Photo: B. Schramm

Western red cedar foliage. Photo: B. Schramm

- **Western red cedar:** The branches are flattened and the needles are scale-like, almost braided looking.

Left: Cedar trees often have snags at the top ideal for birds. Photo: B. Schramm

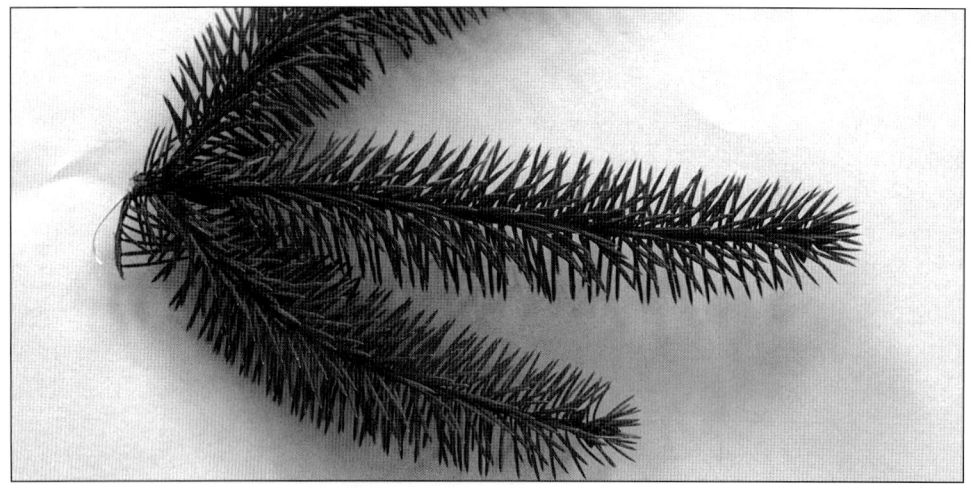

Sitka spruce needles. Photo: Wendy Szaniszlo

- **Sitka spruce:** The branches hold sharp, stiff needles. Grab a branch with your hands; if you say "ouch!" it's a Sitka spruce!

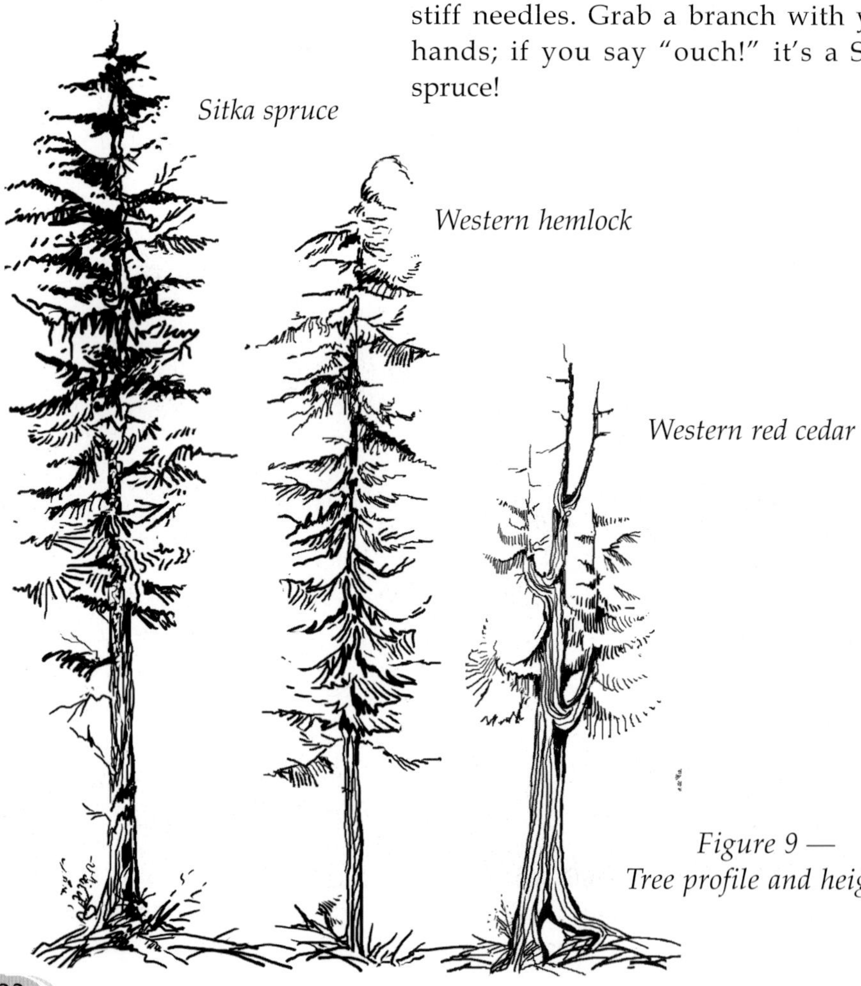

Sitka spruce

Western hemlock

Western red cedar

Figure 9 —
Tree profile and heights

Cedar trees were used by the Nuu-chah-nulth people for canoes and many other uses. Copyright PRNPR Archives.

Rescue skills should be learned in advance of your trip. Photo: Wendy Szaniszlo

Trip preparation checklist

SKILLS

You should be able to:

- Perform basic paddle strokes
- Perform assisted rescues
- Perform self-rescues
- Provide basic first aid
- Read a chart
- Read tide tables
- Interpret marine weather forecasts
- Use a compass with proficiency
- Use a VHF radio

Safety Equipment

- Cell phone
- VHF radio
- GPS (with extra batteries)
- Waterproof cases for electronic accessories
- Chart and chart case
- Tide tables
- Compass
- Flares
- Whistle
- Watch
- Hand-operated pump
- Extra food for one day
- First aid kit
- Hand sanitizer with alcohol
  (To avoid making other people sick, wash your hands!)
- Watertight sprayskirt
- Wetsuit or dry suit
- Personal Flotation Device (PFD)
- Paddle float
- Tow line
- Stirrup (for getting back into kayak from the water)
- Spare paddle

Repair Kit

- Plastic cable ties (tie wraps)
- Tuck Tape
- Duct Tape
- Spare cable nuts for the rudder
- Copper wire
- Small pliers
- Leatherman multi-tool

PERSONAL CLOTHING

Note: Do not bring cotton, and pack your belongings in drybags!

- Footwear for paddling
- Footwear for walking on land
- Socks
- Underwear
- Swimsuit
- Quick-drying pants
- Warm fleece pants
- Short- and long-sleeved shirts
- Light sweater
- Heavy sweater
- Paddling jacket
- Rain gear (top and bottom)
- Sun hat
- Wool hat or toque

CAMPING EQUIPMENT

- Synthetic sleeping bag (not down) in a drybag
- Sleeping pad (e.g. Therm-a-Rest™)
- Tent
- Two tarps, 4 x 4 m (13 x 13 ft)
- Cups, utensils, bowls and pot set
- Stove and fuel
- Lighters or waterproof matches
- Rope and twine
- Water containers or bladders
- Water bottle

PERSONAL ACCESSORIES

- Paddling gloves
- Binoculars
- Books, journal
- Camera

- Headlamp with spare batteries
- Contact lenses or spare prescription glasses (with safety cord)
- Sunglasses with safety cord
- Insect repellent (in spring)
- Lip balm
- Sunscreen
- Money, credit card, ID
- Personal medication
- Small towel and toiletries
- Toilet paper
- Sponge for wiping out your kayak

METRIC/IMPERIAL CONVERSION

MILES, KILOMETRES AND NAUTICAL MILES

1.15 statute (land) mile = 1 nautical mile

1 statute mile = 1.6 km

1.85 km = 1 nautical mile

CENTIMETRES AND INCHES

2.5 cm = 1 inch

30 cm = 1 foot or 12 inches

KILOGRAMS AND POUNDS

1 kg = 2.2 pounds

0.45 kg = 1 pound

1 (metric) tonne = 2,200 pounds or 1,000 kg

TEMPERATURE

Celsius	Fahrenheit
30	86
25	77
20	68
15	59
10	50
5	41
0	32
−5	23

Jean-François (JF) Marleau. Photo: Wendy Szaniszlo

About the Author

Born and raised in Trois-Rivières, Quebec, Jean-François (JF) moved to Ucluelet, on the west coast of Vancouver Island, in 2001 to work as a kayak guide in the Broken Group Islands. The beauty of the surrounding area and the west coast lifestyle captivated him, and he chose this place as his new home.

JF has taught kayaking and guiding expeditions across Canada since 1998. He is a certified Full Guide and Guide Trainer, as well as vice-president, of the Sea Kayak Guides Alliance of BC (SKGABC). He is a certified instructor and has a Level 4 Skills certificate with Paddle Canada. With his partners, he runs SKILS, Canada's leading paddle sports training and consulting business.

When he his not kayaking, JF works as a human resources management consultant for HR Strategik Consulting in British Columbia and Quebec. He is a Certified Human Resources Professional (CHRP). He is also the owner of Pacific Rim Informative Adventures (PRIA), which offers private kayaking courses and develops innovative products to enhance the outdoor recreational experience. JF holds many diplomas, including a Master's degree in Industrial Relations and a Bachelor of Arts degree in Political Science from Laval University (Quebec).

REFERENCE MATERIAL

Arima, E.Y., Denis St.Claire, Louis Clamhouse, Joshua Edgar, Charles Jones and John Thomas. 1991. *Between Ports Alberni and Renfrew: Notes on West Coast Peoples*. Hull: Canadian Museum of Civilization.

Earth Tech (Canada) Inc. 2002. Prideaux Island Dump Site, Pacific Rim National Park, British Columbia. Document prepared for Public Works & Government Services Canada.

Gordon, David, G. 1994. *The Audubon Society Field Guide to the Bald Eagle*. Seattle: Sasquatch Books.

Hatler David F., Wayne Campbell and Adrian Dorst. 1978. *Occasional Papers of the British Columbia Museum*, No. 20, Birds of Pacific Rim National Park, British Columbia.

Inglis, Richard I., and James C. Haggarty. 1986. *Pacific Rim National Park Ethnographic History*. Calgary: Parks and Environment Canada.

MacFarlane J.M., H.J. Quan, K.K. Uyeda, K.D. Wong. 1996. *Official Guide to Pacific Rim Reserve*. Vancouver: Mitchell Press Limited.

McMillan, Alan D. and Denis E. St.Claire. 2003. *Ts'ishaa: Archaeology and Ethnography of a Nuu-Chah-Nulth Origin Site in Barkley Sound. Report of the Tseshaht Archaeological Project, 1999 to 2001*. Prepared for Parks Canada and Tseshaht Nation.

McMillan, Alan D. and Denis E. St.Claire. 1982. *Alberni Prehistory, Archaeological and Ethnographic Investigations on Western Vancouver Island*. Penticton: Theytus Books

Obee, Bruce. 1998. *The Pacific Rim Explorer. The Outdoor Guide*. North Vancouver: Whitecaps Books.

Pacific Rim National Park Reserve. 2002. *Commercial Kayaking Low Impact Activity Guidelines for Pacific Rim National Park Reserve*. Ucluelet: Pacific Rim National Park Reserve.

Peterson, Jan. 1999. *Journey down the Alberni Canal to Barkley Sound*. Lantzville: Oolichan Books.

Pojar, Jim and Andy Mackinnon. 1994. *Plants of Coastal British Columbia including Washington, Oregon & Alaska*. B.C. Ministry of Forests and Lone Pine Publishing.

Randall, Brenda Carleigh. 2000. *An Examination of Visitor Management Issues Within the Broken Group Islands, Pacific Rim National Park Reserve*. Master's Degree Thesis. Malaspina University College.

Scott, R. Bruce. 1972. *Barkley Sound, a history of the Pacific Rim National Park area*. Victoria: Fleming-Review Printing Ltd.

Sea Kayak Instruction & Leadership Systems (SKILS). 2005. *Navigation Notes*. Victoria: SKILS

Sea Kayak Instruction & Leadership Systems (SKILS). 2005. *Weather and Sea State Notes*. Victoria: SKILS

St.Claire, Denis. NA. *Talking About Tseshaht Land History*. Prepared for the Tseshaht First Nation. Coast Heritage Consulting.

Walbran, John T. 1971. *British Columbia Coast Names. Their Origin and History*. Vancouver: Douglas & McIntyre

Wallbank, Jean Buck. 1991. *Benson Island*. Mission (BC): Digital Communication Inc.

White, Brian P. 1974. *Pacific Rim National Park: human history study, volume 1*. Report on file. Ottawa: National and Historic Parks Branch, Department of Indians and Northern Affairs.

" In wildness is the
preservation of the earth"

- Henry David Thoreau